D0616471

THE GOOD SEED

by
Marianna Slocum
with
Grace Watkins

Promise Publishing Company
Orange, California

Cover Design by Mary Chapeau
Photo by Art Zippel
M. B. Steele, Editor
THE GOOD SEED
© 1988 by Promise Publishing Company
Published by Promise Publishing Company
Orange, California 92668
Printed in the United States of America

Library of Congress
Cataloging-in-Publication Data
Slocum, Marianna
The Good Seed
ISBN 0-939497-09-3

Table of Contents

Foreword

"I am with you daily in prayer.
I believe God will use this story
in a wonderful way."

- Uncle Cam Townsend

Dedicated

to my beloved sister,

Dorothy Johnson,

who has
"strengthened my hands in God"
through all the years.

O God, wert Thou ploughing
Thy profitless earth
With the brave plough of Love
And the sharp plough of Pain?

But hark to the mirth
Of wheat field in harvest!

Dear Plougher, well worth
That ploughing, this yellow-gold grain.

Amy Carmichael

CHRONOLOGY

• 1938

Bill Bentley attends the fifth session of Camp Wycliffe; begins work with the Tzeltal Indians in the state of Chiapas, Mexico.

• 1940

Marianna Slocum attends Camp Wycliffe; assigned to the Chol Indians in Chiapas, Mexico.

• 1941, August 24

Bill Bentley dies of a heart attack just days before the wedding; Marianna returns to Mexico to continue his work among the Tzeltals.

• 1941, November

Marianna and Ethel Wallis are refused entrance to Bachajon Tzeltal territory.

• 1944, June

Marianna and Ethel allocated in Yochib, among the highland Oxchuc Tzeltals.

• 1947, January 2

Florence Gerdel, R.N., joins Marianna in Yochib.

• 1949, October

At the request of the new Tzeltal believers, Florence and Marianna move to Corralito.

• 1950, summer

Templo built in Corralito.

• 1951, August 6

Templo in Corralito burned down by those opposed to the Gospel.

- 1951, August 6

  Templo rebuilt in time for civil marriages of 225 couples.

- 1951, August 12

  The Tzeltal church comes into being; first baptisms; elders and deacons ordained.

- 1955-56

  Two-story clinic built by believers in Corralito.

- 1955, August 10

  First martyr; Sebastian of Tenango.

- 1956, August 6

  Dedication of Oxchuc Tzeltal New Testament.

- 1957, April

  Marianna and Florence enter Bachajon Tzeltal territory, scene of former rejection.

- 1963, June

  Completion of New Testament in the Bachajon dialect.

- 1964, September

  Marianna and Florence begin work among the Paez Indians of Colombia, South America.

- 1965, May

  Dedication of Bachajon Tzeltal New Testament.

- 1980, October

  Paez New Testament off the press.

- 1985, May

  Marianna and Florence return to visit Tzeltals with Paez pastor from Colombia, S.A.; filming of "The Good Seed."

Holding forth the Word of Life. . .
Philippians 2:16

The sound of feet running hard
and an urgent cry in Tzeltal
interrupted Bill Bentley
at his makeshift desk
deep in the pine country
of southern Mexico.

The young Indian lad
was gasping for breath
from his rapid pace.

"Come! Come, quickly!

Pancho has been hurt!

Help him!"

Chapter One

First in Chiapas

Bill dropped his pen, grabbed up a small first aid kit and dashed out the door only one step behind the Tzeltal boy who had summoned him. Up a steep incline they ran, past cornfields just beginning to tassel, till they reached a clearing where a few Indian huts were huddled together.

A crowd had gathered already, speaking in heated tones. Bill caught a few of the phrases.

"Drunk"..."*machete*"..."went fleeing."

Bill ducked his head as he entered the smoky little Tzeltal house. The wind rattled the reed walls in a dismal dirge. Pancho hunched in a corner, his clothes bloodied, his head wrapped in dirty rags through which a bright red seeped. At his feet burned a candle. Bill gave an awkward greeting to the young wife who knelt anxiously by her husband's side but she did not reply or look up.

Even before Bill unwrapped the headcovering, a wave of nausea swept over him. Before his unaccustomed eyes gaped an ugly six-inch wound made by the slash of a *machete*. Part of Pancho's brain was exposed through the cranium and the separated bones pulsed with every throb of the victim's artery.

Bill had had a little medical training but nothing to prepare him for this. In his small first aid satchel were a pair of scissors, some gauze, a roll of tape and a bottle of antiseptic. Aware that any treatment of such an injury was exceedingly dangerous, the young North American had no help to offer but to try to assuage the pain. He tried to find the words to ask for boiled water but no one seemed to understand what he wanted. Gingerly, restraining the gagging in his own throat, he cut away the matted hair and washed the wound with antiseptic. Pancho was still inebriated from his weekend debauchery and he only cried out a few times. Bill wished he could feel as stoic as his patient seemed. His hands trembled in sympathy while he muttered a few comforting phrases in what Tzeltal he knew. Pancho's wife, distraught, offered no assistance. Indeed, there was little she could give. A scrawny dog rubbed against his master's feet and two young children whimpered at their mother's knee. The fire in the corner of the dark room had nearly died out when Bill straightened and stretched his taut shoulders. He wanted to give the little family some assurance but he could find no words except in Spanish,

   "*Qué lástima!*"

If they understood, they gave no indication. The small group of onlookers began to drift away.

Bill had been in the state of Chiapas, Mexico, only a few months, trying to learn the language of the Bachajon Tzeltals (batch-a-HONE sell-TALLS). It was a difficult unwritten Mayan language, but even more difficult was the hostility of the people. These lowland Tzeltals, descendants of the ancient Mayans, were noted for their fierceness. Even government agents feared to infringe upon their territory.

Mistreated for centuries by foreign invaders, they resolutely determined to keep to themselves. Laws against murder were no deterrent. Bill was well aware that he took his life in his hands to enter Bachajon. Whenever he had attempted to visit in their small villages or call upon anyone in their homes, he was met with rude antagonism. Not once had he been made to feel welcome.

He had rented a room from a German family who owned a *finca* (coffee plantation) a day's journey from Bachajon territory. Here he came into contact with a few Bachajon men who worked on the plantation and he was able to pick up some Tzeltal phrases from them. Pancho had been the most willing of the plantation workers to help him with Tzeltal words but they had barely begun to make some progress and now he lay dying. The call to aid Pancho had been the first acknowledgement of a need for his help any Indian had given Bill and he knew that was only because no *shaman* (medicine man) was in the vicinity.

Twice each day Bill climbed the steep hill to Pancho's hut, stopping to rest on the way. Sharp pains in his chest were a reminder of a childhood weakness. Coffee trees, just beginning to burst into delicate white blossoms, formed a pleasant shield from the hot sun. Lazy white clouds floated idly in a sky of lapis lazuli. Gentle winds riffled his dark brown hair. In spite of the gravity of his errand, Bill delighted in the beauty that was distinctively southern Mexico. He understood why the Tzeltals defended their borders so fiercely from encroachers for it was a land of splendid contrast, each color vying with the next in depth and loveliness. In the few months he had lived in the state of Chiapas, he had learned to love it intensely.

Each time he visited Pancho, he attempted to converse with the young wife but he was met by stolid passivity. Frustration filled him for he had a desperate need to speak with those about him. Instead, all he could do was to wash out the wound and check for infection. There was little in the hut to alleviate the pain of the wounded man. A stark plank bed covered with a thin woven mat provided little comfort for his aching body. Three large stones in a corner comprised the family cooking area. No other furniture graced this typical Indian home, not even a table or chair.

On the third day, there was a faint odor of decay and Bill realized his patient had little chance of recovery. Pancho could speak clearly and did so, frequently threatening to chop his antagonist and his entire family to pieces. Delirium seized Pancho and the young wife sent the children off to another hut to keep them from his irrational threatenings. Within a week, infection had reached Pancho's brain and his left side became paralyzed. Then his speech left him and he slipped into unconsciousness. For four days more he lingered, shallow breathing the only sign of life. The Indians confided in Bill that Pancho's soul was visiting all those to whom he had done evil (he had killed three or four men in drunken fights). When he finally died in the evening of the thirteenth day, a surprising sense of loss swept over the young foreigner. He had known this Indian man only slightly before the fight which had brought about his death but he grieved as if he had lost a close friend. He had desperately wanted to give the entire family a Message of Love but he had lacked the words they could comprehend.

Perhaps it was his obvious concern for Pancho which began to penetrate the hearts of some of the Bachajon villagers for an imperceptible change in their attitude toward Bill began. No longer did the men glare at him in hostility when he met them on the pathways nor did the women avert their faces. Occasionally, a child would sidle up to him for a gentle caress. It was only a small beginning but a faint hope began to stir within Bill.

It was 1938. Bill had been in Mexico three months, long enough to sense the enormity of the task before him and to be overwhelmed by it. He had come to bring the Word of God in their own language to people who had never heard of a Savior's love, never known the possibility of forgiveness. And he had not been able to tell them. Their physical and spiritual needs tore at his heart. Surrounded by people who spoke German, Spanish, Chol and Tzeltal, Bill found himself isolated completely from anyone who talked or even thought as he did. He was a foreigner in a foreign culture.

Though he was a gifted musician, he owned no musical instrument, not even a radio. The Depression was at its height in the States and the only support he received was $10 monthly from a Sunday School class in his home church in Topeka, Kansas. Mail was undependable and his location was almost inaccessible. Time after time, he would travel two hours through mud and heavy rain to the nearest town to find no letters from family or friends. Loneliness gnawed at him when he was least expecting it. And yet, it never occurred to him to feel sorry for himself. Joy filled his life in the most mundane of tasks and he found himself singing lustily as he walked the trails of Bachajon.

To the Indians about him, he was something of an enigma. Accustomed as they had been to exploitation, they found his open friendliness cause for suspicion in itself. Since Tzeltal men considered anyone who sat at a desk "looking at paper" all day incredibly lazy, Bill went out to the fields with them and worked, sometimes raking the coffee beans to keep them drying evenly, sometimes recording the number of bags each man brought in. He laughed with them, tried to talk with them, but mostly he listened. He drank their *posol* (corn gruel) and ate their food, paying the price for it later with bouts of amoeba and parasites of every kind.

In the evening, he puzzled over the phrases he had heard that day, trying to decipher the grammar and distinctive tones of the Tzeltal language. The next day, at work with the men on the plantation, he tried out his newest phrases. If they were understood, he decided to keep them in his files. If they were not, he tried again. Gradually, the language began to come to him. Methodically, he wrote down what he thought he heard, revising, checking, testing. Frustration and impatience were his steady companions.

For three years, Bill tramped the trails of Bachajon, trying to gain an entrance into Tzeltal territory where he could settle and feel a part of their lives. He realized he could never truly serve the Indians unless he understood them and he could not understand them unless he lived among them. He needed a more thorough grasp of the language before he could begin the translation work so vital to bringing God's Word to the Chiapas Indians. Though the incident with Pancho had reduced their antagonism toward him, they still had not developed enough warmth toward the foreigner to allow him permanent entrance into their villages. With Juan, a trusted language helper, Bill penetrated firther and further into the Bachajon territory, feeling more and more skilled with his use of their language. Some of his trips lasted weeks and he would return to the German ranch thoroughly exhausted.

Ordinarily, he avoided villages where a *fiesta* was in progress for the heavy drinking often created nasty fights. However, one day he and Juan had been walking for eleven hours when they came upon a Bachajon village. The pain in his chest was beginning to give him warning signals. The boom of skyrockets punctuated the plaintive wail of flutes and the erratic beat of drums. He would have passed by but he was too weary to walk any further. He realized he could never gain the attention of any officials during such revelry so he leaned against a tree, exhaustion permeating every muscle in his body. His eyes followed a narrow horse trail leading to a massive stone church around which a few thatched huts were clustered. A town hall and a government boarding school were the only other buildings in this small outpost for most of the people in the area dwelt in the forest, huts hidden from view.

Oblivious of the foreigner, a procession of handsome, bronze-skinned Indians were parading around the village. The women wore off-the-shoulder embroidered blouses, bright ribbons in their black braids, the men were in white muslin shirts with rows of bright blue buttons decorating the throat opening. In a low voice, to avoid attracting attention, Juan informed him that this was the Feast of San Miguel.

At the edge of the group sprawled a dozen forms sodden with drink. A mob of men and women, only slightly less drunk, trooped behind a blue-draped figure of their patron saint. It tipped dangerously from side to side as four men bore it on their shoulders before setting it down in front of one of the tall crosses encircling the village. Bill and Juan watched for a while, then turned back. Disappointment once again faced them.

Suddenly their way was blocked. On edge because of the ever-present threat to their lives, Bill and Juan stood still, waiting. A stocky middle-aged Indian man with a weathered face and imposing air of authority headed a group of Tzeltals who seemed aware of the foreigner in their midst for the first time. Bill could not tell from their expressions if they were belligerent or simply curious. Their dispositions were volatile and could turn from indifference to hostility in a flash. In mutilated but unmistakable English, the leader asked,

"Is it true, sir, that in your land you have a Book from God?"

Bill was startled. The query seemed out of place in the middle of the ribaldry of the moment. Before he could reply, the Indian continued with further explanation.

"When I was a soldier, I went as far as the border of your land. There I heard that you have a Book from God. Is that true?"

In Tzeltal, Bill replied, "Why, yes, we do have God's Book in my land."

A curious crowd had joined the others, attracted by the novelty of a foreigner speaking the "real language" (their own).

Miguel de Mesa, tattered and disheveled from the three-day religious festival, was pleased with himself for having asked the question in English and for having been so readily understood. He ventured another.

"Do you have this Book from God?"

"Yes, I have the Book," Bill answered. "I am learning your language so that I can give you God's Book in your own language."

Miguel turned excitedly to the crowd gathered about them. In rapid Tzeltal, he explained the idea which had come to him, then turned back to Bill.

"Why don't you come live here? Bring the Book from God so that you can tell us what it says."

Bill could not believe his ears. After all this time and in the most unlikely of situations, the deepest desire of his heart was about to be realized - an invitation to dwell in Bachajon territory. He knew he had to be cautious. With his heart pounding, he answered Miguel in a hesitant reminder,

"We would have to ask permission of the town officials."

"Oh, yes," Miguel agreed. He turned to his Tzeltal friends. There was a short conversation but Bill could ascertain no dissent. It was the first group of villagers who had given even the slightest hint of welcoming him and his mind could not quite take it in.

He and Juan found a shelter for the night, wearily unrolling their mats on the earth floor, grateful for a place to rest. Most of the night, the sound of festivities continued to bombard their ears. Juan slept right through it. Bill dozed fitfully, waking occasionally to allow his mind to race ahead. If he actually did get permission to build a house near this village, he could begin to concentrate on the translation. Besides that, he and Marianna would have a place to begin their married life right in the midst of the people to whom they felt God's call so strongly.

The last skyrocket was eventually fired, the last flute gave its final tune and the last drumroll finished almost unheard. The village was asleep.

In the morning, true to his word, Miguel summoned the town secretary for a meeting with the *trensipals* (town officials). Bill presented a letter of recommendation from the Head of Indian Affairs in Mexico City which had been written for him earlier. The *trensipals*, though they could not read, were impressed by the official seal on the document. Solemnly, the old men of the village agreed to allow Bill to establish a home in the village. Elated, thrilled and humbled simultaneously, Bill lifted a grateful heart to the Lord with the words of his favorite hymn, "Great Is Thy Faithfulness." Three years of preparation and perseverance had begun to reveal signs of hope.

*Except a grain of wheat
fall into the ground and die,
it abideth alone;
but if it die,
it beareth much fruit.*
John 12:24

Camp Wycliffe,
Sulphur Springs, Arkansas,
summer of 1940.

Of all the years I have spent,
probably that brief period of time
was the most influential in my life.

Heat, insects, dust, hard work, joy, fun,
and a definite calling
all made up those few months.

And of course, there was Bill Bentley.

Chapter Two

Ambassador To Mexico

I had traveled from Philadelphia by train for three days. Travel weary and dusty, I had arrived on a sticky Saturday afternoon so thirsty I thought my tongue would swell up and drop off. I looked up and there was Evelyn Woodward whom I had known at Wilson College! If either of us had realized the other was going to be at Camp Wycliffe that summer, we could have traveled together! We hugged each other in delight and relief at seeing a familiar face.

Some of the young men already at Camp Wycliffe stood by to help with our suitcases. We who had spent four years at an all women's college found their good-natured joking a lift to our exhausted spirits and we forgot our shyness. Bill Bentley leaned over to pick up my suitcase and our eyes met for one second. I'm sure he didn't notice me in any particular way but I couldn't help noticing him. Tall and pleasant, his laughing brown eyes and cheerful manner made us feel welcome immediately.

We were a small group of students from many parts of the country joined by one compelling interest - that of taking God's Word to people without Him. Camp Wycliffe had been founded only six years before by Cameron Townsend who took as a literal command Christ's injunction to "go into all the world and preach the gospel." He realized the Gospel had to be in the language of the hearers or it would not penetrate their understanding. In obedience to the same command, we young people had gathered at Camp Wycliffe that summer to prepare to be translators. Our lessons in phonology, morphology, syntax (tools for language learning) occupied most of our waking moments but there was time for the lighter side as well - swims in the river, watermelon feasts, long talks and even a romance or two. We laughed, we teased one another, we struggled, and we rejoiced. There I formed some of the deepest friendships of my life.

Our studies were both grueling and challenging. The professors with their brilliant minds, fascinating tales of other cultures and insights into other viewpoints, were dominated by one personality - that of Uncle Cam Townsend. His enthusiasm was irresistible. His excitement penetrated every conversation. And all topics led to Bible translation. We were at the beginning of a tremendous venture for Christ. We sensed the privilege of His call. From that small group of fifty-three students that summer, God's message was to spread to Mexico, Alaska, Central and South America and Africa.

Even among all these young people thoroughly dedicated to the cause of Christ, Bill Bentley stood out. He bore an air of complete confidence in the Lord and a single-mindedness that sparked the rest of us toward the task of translating the Scriptures into unknown tongues. Perseverance was his keynote.

So motivated were we that ten of us did not waste time returning to our homes after the summer study program. Instead, we decided to travel straight to Mexico from Sulphur Springs. Bill and six of the new recruits took only what they had at Camp Wycliffe for luggage, piled it into a truck and set off. My parents, concerned at the thought of their daughter traveling to a foreign country by truck, drove from Philadelphia to Camp Wycliffe, then took two other girls and me on to Mexico City in the family car. We must have been a strange-looking group. Our vehicle was piled high with boxes and suitcases and five adults were crammed into that one small automobile for hours of traveling. But war was threatening and no one traveled by plane. Crossing the Mexican border in those days was simple for no passports were required.

I was twenty-two at the time. Bill, at twenty-six, and already a seasoned veteran with two years' experience in Mexico, provided the background knowledge in travel and language which were indispensable to us. He helped us through customs, found lodgings for us, decided what food was safe to eat.

We fell in love with Mexico City. Exotic, sunny, colorful, it lay like a jewel in a dried lake bed seven thousand feet above sea level. The clear skies and two snow-capped peaks in the distance created a panorama of unrivaled majesty. The climate was perfect; cool in the evenings, warm in the daytime.

My parents lingered a week with us, partly to enjoy the celebration of September 16, Mexico's Independence Day and partly to set their minds at ease over my choice of vocation. It was a difficult leave-taking for them but they had given me to the Lord many years before and they rested in the knowledge of God's call on my life. Throughout the years which followed, my family has been my solid support and their prayers have strengthened the entire work of missions in Mexico.

Up until then, Bill Bentley had not singled me out for any particular attention. He treated all the girls the same - teasing, friendly, interested. I had

fallen in love with him. Everything about him attracted me; his manly good looks, his lovely tenor
singing voice but most captivating of all was his
complete dedication to the work of the Lord. As
leader of our group, he was thoughtful of our
needs, seeming to anticipate them before we even
thought of them. Wherever he went in Mexico, he
had made a practice of walking the trails on foot
for he did not want to take a higher place than the
Indians he came to serve. His beautiful, winsome
smile began to dominate my thoughts.

We headed south to the farthest state in Mexico,
Chiapas. Bill was in charge of allocating the new-
comers. He had located a coffee plantation in the
Chiapas mountains for my partner, Evelyn Woodward, and me to stay while we studied the Chol
language. In response to Bill's request, Stanford
Morison, an American rancher, had extended an
invitation to us to begin our studies at the Alianza ranch, where he lived with his Mexican wife and
their six children. Mary, their oldest daughter,
had reached an age where she needed companion-
ship and intellectual stimulation. It was partly for
this reason as well as from a genuine sense of
hospitality that the Morison family invited us to
make the Alianza our home for a few months.
They gave us a tiny house of boards with a tin roof,
an unobstructed view of craggy mountains in the
distance and a merry little stream running behind.
The town of Tumbala was within walking distance.
There a small congregation of Chol Indians held
services in pure Chol. We became anxious to get
God's written Word to them in their own language.

Evy was particularly burdened for the Chols.
She had always been an outstanding language
student at Wilson College where she and I had
struck up an enduring friendship. Tall and placid

with a circlet of brown braids about her head, she was an excellent companion and partner for me. Though she had originally intended to go to India as a missionary, she recognized the need of the Chol Indians while at Camp Wycliffe and was among the first to volunteer to go straight to Mexico without returning home. Together, we tackled the very beginnings of learning the Chol language though, in the back of my mind, I sometimes wondered if I should not be studying Tzeltal instead!

Bill had begun to visit us occasionally even though it was a seven-hour walk for him from the German coffee plantation where he had lived for two years. I looked forward to his visits more than I ever wanted to admit at the time.

Our hosts, the Morisons, were a delightful family. Stanford, a Yale graduate, had chosen Mexico for his home even though the financial rewards had not been particularly great. Elodia, his Mexican wife, was busy from morning to night with duties about the coffee plantation as well as tending to her large family.

The children kept our days lively and interesting but outstanding among them was charming seventeen-year-old Mary. She loved being around us and we loved having her. She was curious about everything American and kept us smiling with her outspoken comments. But when we started a Bible class for the children, she was not interested in attending. She had more exciting things to do!

There could be no lovelier scenery than in the Chiapas mountains. The picturesque trails led through groves of bananas, sugar cane patches, thatched huts. It was an ideal climate with clear warm sunlight and blue skies filled with white clouds and brief afternoon rains to wash the countryside. My love for Mexico has never left me.

Bill had made it clear from the very first that he was not interested in romance for its own sake but was concerned only with God's will in his choice of a wife. I'll never forget the day, January 6, 1941, when I received his letter carried by an Indian messenger saying he was now certain I was God's choice for him. Secretly, I had hoped for this but actually to be the wife of Bill Bentley was almost more than I could comprehend! I was thrilled; I was excited; I was humbled. A man so staunch for God demanded a wife equally committed in her pursuit of His perfect will for both of them and equally called to the ministry. Of necessity, letters took the place of personal visits. The red-white-and-green Mexican mail sacks tied on the backs of reluctant mules became the bearers of good tidings. Sometimes, affable Mexican ranchers who happened along carried them for us; even, occasionally, the *henequen* net bag of a trustworthy Indian brought precious news between us. Distance separated us and it drew us close at the same time in a longing for the future when we could truly be together for the rest of our lives.

Twice in February, Bill came to visit; the first time to bring Uncle Cam who wanted to get acquainted with our situation as well as with our hosts at the Alianza. He grasped immediately the distinctive quality in seventeen-year-old Mary Morison and stated in his visionary way,

"That girl needs more schooling. She has a lot of potential."

We felt the same way.

The second visit was more cause for celebration for it was on February 14. In a box of cookies baked by Bill's German hostess, lay a large, heart-shaped cookie especially for me. We were officially engaged! I was more excited than I could express. Bill's engagement gift to me was a perfectly carved jade head that had possibly been a pendant worn around the neck of some proud long-vanished Mayan chieftain.

In his first letter after our official engagement, Bill wrote,

Is it only I, or do all men begin with difficulty to open their hearts to another other than the Lord? In spite of constant kidding, hinting, etc., from others, I have always left "love" to the Lord's perfect will but I didn't imagine He would bring "the one" here instead of sending me after her.

Looking to the Lord in His Word about this, He turned my thoughts to Ephesians 5:25 on the trail home. How does Christ operate in love for His Church? He joins, first, two into one spirit. Then, He joins the soul as we learn to know each other in heart. I tremble to think of the pattern I should fulfill: The Bridegroom and His love for the Bride - He "who loved her and gave Himself for her."

In the meantime, there was concentrated language study to be continued if either the Tzeltals or the Chols were to have the Word of God. As dry season began, Bill ventured into the vast, forbidding Bachajon region. These Indians were fiercely independent, hostile to strangers, even those of another Indian tribe, and antagonistic to any outside influence. They wanted to preserve their own traditions, uncontaminated by foreigners. Yet, it was to these Tzeltals that Bill felt called to bring the Gospel of Jesus Christ. With Juan, his faithful informant, Bill took along the newly-translated Gospel of John to share with the Bachajon Tzeltals. A week's journey on foot brought them to a village where thirty Tzeltals gathered to hear Juan explain the Word, sing a few hymns in Tzeltal and pray with them.

I could almost see Bill grinning as he wrote,

It was very amusing that way back there in the woods with only thatched-roofed, mud-walled huts for miles and miles of mountains, there were two old victrolas, the kind with huge horns. Of course, they had to be played and played for our entertainment. And among the half-dozen records was Lohengrin's Wedding March!

Bill took longer than usual to rest up from this journey. In spite of the good care that doña Emilia, his German hostess, gave him, his strength was taxed. And still, he had not found a site for a home for us where we could readily live among these Bachajon Tzeltals. Though I longed to have him visit me at the Alianza, he decided to take another trip into Bachajon territory to try once more.

He was gone a week on his next trip. Returning even more weary than before, he still managed to summon strength to write me again, this time with the joyful news that he had found a place for us to settle and learn Tzeltal fluently enough to give God's Word to this untaught tribe. He had met Miguel de Mesa, the weather-beaten old *trensipal* who had inquired of the "Book from God," then invited Bill to come build a house among them and teach them what God's Book said!

It was exciting, exhilarating and sobering. I found it increasingly difficult to concentrate on language studies, especially since I would be working with the Tzeltal, not the Chol Indians.

Our marriage plans began to take shape. August 30, 1941 was to be our wedding day and the place would be my parents' home in Ardmore, Pennsylvania. However, first we planned to attend another summer session at Camp Wycliffe in Sulphur Springs and stop off in Topeka, Kansas for a visit with Bill's family before going on to my home in Pennsylvania.

Uncle Cam had asked us to consider taking Mary Morison along with us for an education and exposure to good Christian teaching. He was positive that after my marriage, she would make an excellent partner for Evelyn even though the girl did not yet indicate any interest in spiritual matters for herself, let alone for the Indians of Mexico! Such was Uncle Cam's faith; he never saw the obstacles, only the possibilities.

Evy and I were reluctant at first. We had planned to fly as far as Las Casas but there would not be enough funds for air fare for all of us. There was no money in the Morison household to pay for travel expenses to the States. But we had learned not to question Uncle Cam's vision. After praying about it, we decided to include Mary in our plans for there was little possibility of her receiving an education if she remained on the ranch for the rest of her life. The three of us agreed to pool our funds to stretch for four. It was barely enough. We had to change our mode of travel from a small plane flight to a three-day journey on horseback.

"This will be a good opportunity for us to see the Lord work for Mary as He has for us," I suggested, as much to reassure myself as anything.

In one of his last letters to me before we left for our much-anticipated trip to the States, Bill wrote,

Darling, have you put me on the altar of sacrifice if He so chooses? He must be glorified, His will done.

Then, in a quote from Amy Carmichael, he concluded,

If I forget that the way of the Cross leads to the Cross and not to a bank of flowers....

And, from a favorite hymn,

In a love which cannot cease, I am yours, and you are mine,

Bill.

Brainerd Legters, who was to be Bill's best man at the wedding, joined us for the trip to Las Casas overland. He was a translator working among the Maya in Yucatan. His broad smile and huge sense of adventure added a dimension of excitement to our party.

In high spirits, the five of us set out from the ranch one glorious day in May, exhilarated by the rain-washed freshness of the early morning air. Everything was alive and vibrant. An occasional Indian passed on the trail, sweat trickling down his bronzed face, his calf muscles bulging with the weight of the unhusked corn on his back. Along this trail, I viewed my first Bachajon Tzeltals; a long line of vigorous, muscular Indian men, erect and proud with long sheathed *machetes* swinging from their hips.

Ominous clouds began to pile up overhead. Fruitlessly, we urged our horses on with a jab of our heels and a flick of our whips. Nothing hurried them. The dry season in Chiapas was ending.

A sudden, violent shower drenched us all. Bill had no raincoat and was quickly soaked to the skin. In a couple of hours, we arrived at a small village where it seemed obvious there was no place to stay. Bill talked to a family who took pity on our bedraggled forms and vacated a room for us girls. Bill, dressed in a pair of Brainerd's pajamas, dried his sodden clothes over a smoky open fire. He could have passed for a real Indian!

The trail next day was even worse. Rugged paths like corkscrews wound up and up and we frequently lost sight of Bill and Brainerd who took advantage of steeper shortcuts while our horses stuck to the main trail. By late afternoon, we had reached the desolate village of Cancuc (Can-CUC) perched precariously on the crest of a mountain which dropped suddenly to a turbulent river below. The Cancuc Tzeltals had a reputation for drunkenness and killing. As we rode through the village, women in dirty, loose *huipils* (handwoven, knee-length dresses) retreated inside their smoke-blackened huts. Unkempt youngsters stared sullenly at us. Drunken men with black staffs in hand glared with open hostility. It was not only from the cold that we shivered. A heavy antagonism permeated the atmosphere. We were relieved when we had passed the last little hut in that village.

Through all the dreary weather and frightening encounters, Mary remained as cheerful and lively as if she were going to a party. This was her first real adventure away from home and she determined to make the most of it! The rest of us were cold and hungry and thirsty. There had been no opportunity to purchase food along the way and what food we had brought from the Alianza was now gone. I tried to roast an egg in the fire but it exploded. The others ate theirs raw. Our sense of humor became a little strained.

An early start next morning brought us to Yochib where a persevering young Mexican schoolteacher and his wife were the only outsiders living among the Oxchuc (Osh-CHUC) Tzeltals. We were able to breakfast on black beans, *tortillas* and thick, sweet Indian-style coffee. It was good to have our stomachs full once again and it certainly raised our spirits!

Beyond Yochib, the trail descended sharply to a makeshift bridge of a few squared logs spanning the river. We dismounted to lead our horses across and to give ourselves a change of posture. Through all this journey, Bill had journeyed on foot because he wanted to be free to talk to the Indians we met about the Lord.

On the far side of the river, a different type of Tzeltal settlement greeted our eyes. The Tenejapa (Ten-e-HAPA) Tzeltals tended neat cornfields along the steep mountain slopes and maintained tidy, squat little huts. More accustomed to strangers than the Cancuc Tzeltals we had encountered the day before, the Tenejapanecos greeted us with a stolid "*con, ta*", as they trotted past us on their way to market. The men and boys wore knee-length black blankets which were belted at the waist and had a slit for their heads, and brightly-embroidered shorts showing underneath. From the peaks of their wide-brimmed hats fluttered many gaily-colored ribbons. The women, with thick braids dangling from under the tumplines across their foreheads, wore embroidered white blouses of coarse weave tucked into long blue skirts with full pleats in front.

We had passed through the entire expanse of Tzeltal territory. We had seen the Bachajon, the Cancuc, the Oxchuc and the Tenejapa Tzeltals each in their distinctive costumes, each desperately needing the Word of God in their respective dialects. Bill and I were more determined than ever to bring "our tribe" the Good News.

Beyond Tenejapa, the terrain turned more rugged yet. We passed sere, eroded flanks of mountains guarded by sentinel pines, a thicket of tall stark crosses marking Indian graves, then the all-Indian country gave way to the outskirts of town. After fourteen weary hours in the saddle that day, we rode into Las Casas just as the setting sun dropped behind the mountain peaks. Even Mary was relieved to take a reprieve from our travels!

Our summer was packed full with travel and wedding plans. We spent a month at Camp Wycliffe, then visited Bill's welcoming family in Topeka. Mary stayed on at Camp Wycliffe where she came to know the Lord that summer. Again, Uncle Cam's vision had preceded reality!

At home in Ardmore, the Slocum family took Bill to their hearts with the same love in which they had enveloped me all my life. We were glad for the comparative quiet for both of us were suffering from ongoing bouts with amoeba. Knowing this, one of the well-meaning ladies in our church suggested to Bill that he could "make a good living" if he remained in the States. His reply was very firm.

"I'm not interested in merely making a living, I want to make a life!"

We were on medication and we felt assured there would be no delay in our return to the Tzeltals immediately following our marriage.

One week before our wedding date, Bill and I were invited to a conference in Keswick, N.J., for the day. Bill moved the hearts of many as he depicted the thousands in our neighboring country who had never once been told of the love of Jesus, who had never had opportunity to hold one word of His message in their hands, who, even today, were dying with no hope. He was able to convey to them the incalculable joy he knew of translating God's Word into a language that truly spoke to their own hearts. The press of people about him, the stress of public speaking, had made him very tired.

Bill had never been to New York City. In spite of the demanding day we had just spent, we took advantage of the Saturday before our wedding to "do the town." We rode to the top of the Empire State Building, and talked of the Tzeltals. We walked around the city, sightseeing, and we talked of the Tzeltals. So involved in our discussion were we that we suddenly found ourselves late for the train that was to take us back to Philadelphia. We ran to make it. On the train, Bill squeezed my hand and whispered,

"This time next week, we'll be married, darling."

"And be on our way to the Tzeltals," I added with a smile.

It was dark when we arrived in Philadelphia but we did stop long enough for Bill to buy some ice cream to take home to my parents.

Sunday morning breakfast in the Slocum household was always a family affair. Bill did not appear and it was getting late. Dad commented quietly,

"Bill must be oversleeping."

"He's probably tired," my mother interjected. "This has been a busy weekend for him."

But time was hastening and we would be late to church. Dad went upstairs to call Bill.

I heard one startled gasp from my father, "He's gone!"

Unbelieving, I dashed into the room. I had never seen a dead person before, but I knew - and I didn't believe it. Bright, laughing, vibrant Bill was gone! It couldn't be and yet it was!

His heart, weakened by a childhood illness and by tramping the trails of Chiapas, had simply worn out. Shock, numbness, overwhelming grief left me completely tearless.

Within an hour, my father had phoned Uncle Cam. In a daze, I asked to speak to him. My voice barely audible, I had one request.

"May I return to the Tzeltals, in Bill's place?"

Without hesitation came Uncle Cam's resounding reply, "Yes!"

From Camp Wycliffe came a telegram later that day with this promise,

What I do thou knowest not now,
but thou shalt know hereafter.
John 13:7

I was to see that promise fulfilled many years later.

I walked in a cloud of numb incomprehension, doing all the things I had to do, allowing my family to make what plans seemed best. All the joy in the future had disintegrated.

His Word, memorized many years before, returned.

Fear not, for I have redeemed thee,
I have called thee by thy name,
thou art mine!
When thou passest through the waters,
I will be with thee.
Isa.43:1-2

In blind faith, I struggled through the dark days
and nights, an ache within I could not describe.
Night and day, it throbbed. But still, I remembered.

He had called me, and He was with me.

No other assurance could have carried me
through those black days. Bill was gone but God's
call still remained. I had no choice nor will but to
answer.

We had a service for Bill in my home the following Wednesday afternoon. Dr. Rowan Pearce who
was to have performed our wedding ceremony, instead brought words of comfort to us at Bill's
memorial service.

Said I not unto thee that,
if thou wouldest believe,
thou shouldest see the glory of God?
John 11:40

On Wednesday night, my brother Walter and I
boarded the train together with Bill's casket and
traveled to Topeka. What was to have been a
glorious celebration of joy had turned into a trail
of dazed sorrow. Uncle Cam conducted the
funeral in Bill's church. That was our loving
farewell to Bill. Surrounded by his family and
friends, I knew only Uncle Cam and Walter. I was
alone...and not alone.

The small gravestone in the Topeka cemetery
bears the inscription,

William C. Bentley 1913-1941
Ambassador for Christ to Mexico

Within a week, I was on my way back to the Tzeltals.

I have chosen you...
that you should go and bring forth fruit.
John 15:16

It was a long day's journey on horseback
from the German ranch
where I had been staying
with my partner, Ethel Wallis,
to the village of Bachajon.

Ken Weathers had come to accompany us
and our hopes were high that morning.
At last, we were on our way
to build a little house
where Bill had already secured permission
in his encounter with Miguel de Mesa
the previous spring.

We had the letters of authorization
from the Department of Indian Affairs
and were looking forward
with great anticipation
to this new venture
to which God had called us.

Chapter Three

Rejection

An hour had not passed since Bill's death that I had not prayed for these same Tzeltals he had loved so greatly. We had not been able to locate Miguel de Mesa to renew friendship with him but we were confident the Lord would provide a good contact once we arrived in Bachajon.

Nothing could have prepared us for the open animosity which met us shortly after dismounting in front of the town hall. The mood of the *trensipals* was ugly. Someone had passed through the village a few days earlier and had warned them of the dangers of entertaining Protestants.

"They will steal your land," they had warned. "They will poison the minds of your children. They will make you leave the old ways."

No matter how calmly and logically Ken tried to persuade the village elders gathered in the dingy town hall, they became more and more angry. We were a threat to their security and they did not want us.

The setback was unbelievable. We were so sure the Lord had directed us to Bachajon. Years of prayer and preparation had gone into this day. Now, we stood before the same *trensipals* Bill had contacted a few months earlier and faced complete hostility.

A long discussion in angry voices had gone on for some time. We understood only a few Tzeltal phrases.

"It isn't good."

"We don't want them."

And, worst of all, a vehement accusation, "They are Protestants!"

While we stood and watched, the *trensipals* drew up an official protest to the governor of the state of Chiapas, saying they did not want us in their village. They all affixed their thumbprints to this document. It was final. We were denied permission. There was even the threat that if we tried to make a home here, they would nail our door shut and burn down the house.

The Bachajon Indians had good cause to fear outsiders. Previous white people had cruelly exploited them, taken their land, burned their saints. They had no real reason to trust us.

Heartsick, for the first time in my life, I realized what rejection was.

> *He came unto His own,*
> *and His own received Him not.*
> John 1:11

One discouragement followed another. Sometimes it seemed as though I were moving through uncharted ways, gray mist all about me, no clear path to follow. The months succeeding Bill's death had passed in a blur of sorrow, resignation, acceptance and the resolve to keep our commitment to the Tzeltals.

Attempts to settle in various areas in Tzeltal territory met with repeated rebuffs. I continued my study of the language at the same ranch Bill had made his headquarters while I made effort after effort to locate a settlement where I could be among the people Bill had so dearly loved.

There seemed no welcome for me or the Word of God in either high or low country. It was a time of great testing. Perhaps He needed to do some "translating" in me, before He could use me to do the translation for the Tzeltals. Many times I turned back to the passage where God was assuring His people,

Behold, I send an Angel before thee,
to keep thee in the way,
and to bring thee into the place
which I have prepared.

Exodus 23:20

Ethel Wallis had joined me as an off-and-on partner in November of 1941. She spoke Spanish fluently. Practical and fun-loving, Ethel craved excitement. With an active mind and outgoing personality, she was good company for me.

We remained at the German ranch and continued our study of Tzeltal with renewed vigor. We had no permanent home yet but someday we would!

Then, one afternoon at a "casual" social encounter in Las Casas, we met two noted anthropologists, Dr. Sol Tax of the University of Chicago and Professor Alfonso Villa Rojas of the Carnegie Institution. When they heard that Ethel and I were doing linguistic work with the Tzeltals, they became extremely interested. Villa told us "these high-country Indians are a 'fossil' of the ancient Mayan culture," the only thing of its kind existent anywhere in the hemisphere today! The two men asked us to keep notes of the anthropological customs of the Tzeltals. We agreed to do so, flattered that two such eminent scientists would entrust such research to us!

From that meeting, many months later, arose an offer from Villa to turn over a little house he had built in Yochib to us for six months.

I remembered Yochib. We five had breakfasted there with a Mexican schoolteacher and his wife after our hungry night camping out on the way back to the States for our wedding. There was nothing there but a schoolhouse. And still, we had been looking for over two years. Even if the house was offered for only six months, it was a partly-opened door to the high-country Tzeltals!

Yochib has very few trees but there was an orange tree in the front yard of this one-room house which was to become our home. It was on a steep mountainside and within a few hundred yards ran the main trail between high country and low country.

Professor Villa was an intense, highly intelligent man with dark snapping eyes and a keen, intuitive understanding of Indians. He had studied under the renowned American anthropologist, Robert Redfield, at the University of Chicago. When he returned to teach in Mexico, he found himself particularly fascinated by the Oxchuc Tzeltals. On the front of the house where he had done his field investigation for the past two years hung a sign:

> Center of Ethnographical Studies
> affiliated with
> The Carnegie Institution
> of Washington

I had never lived in such a prestigious-sounding dwelling!

Professor Villa left us what little he had in the way of furniture. We slept in sleeping bags on folding Army cots. Our washbasin sat on two wooden boxes which we turned outward for shelves. For light, we used a gasoline pressure lamp and a two-burner gasoline stove for cooking. When my only pen disappeared from the table right under the open window, we learned to keep our few precious belongings out of sight.

The most important heritage willed to us by Villa was his friendship with the Indians. From the first day, the Oxchuc Indians, poorest of all the Tzeltals, made a path to our door. We gave them simple medicines for their many illnesses and we learned from them. Their dialect was different from that of the lowland Tzeltals which I had been studying the past three years.

"What is that?" I would ask, pointing to my informant's hair.

"*Stsotsil jol*" (A blanket for my head) would come the reply.

Laboriously, I repeated what I heard, trying to analyze the sounds into symbols which could then be written down on index cards and filed. I immersed myself in learning the language, spoken in the context of the life of the Indians all around me. Whenever I heard a new word, I recorded it on a 3x5 card, added it to the growing number of words in the dictionary I was compiling and used it in actual speech to store it in my memory. This Mayan language fascinated me! Passed down from their ancestors, they had a fully-developed numerical system, counting by twenties from one to sixty-four million, without a single loan word from Spanish!

Sometimes, when I felt confident I had mastered

a phrase, I would discover it was wrong in some detail and again, we would start from the beginning. Many a time I thought it would have been easier to have been born an Oxchuc Tzeltal!

Ethel was with me for that first summer in Yochib, then she went on to another ministry.

One of my greatest hardships was the sense of loneliness I experienced when I had no partner. Sometimes I would go as long as seven weeks without hearing a word of English spoken. This provided an excellent atmosphere for learning Tzeltal but the sense of isolation from the familiar lurked at the back of my mind. Yochib was over thirty miles from Las Casas, the main city of the area. Even on horseback, it was a full day's journey. Since the mountain trail was so rugged, I never attempted it on foot. There were no horses in Yochib. If I needed one, I would have to send a message to Las Casas by an Indian on his way to market, then wait for him to bring a horse on his return.

Mail delivery was always chancy, depending on the passing of a pack train or a willing Tzeltal coming past my house. There was no radio at Yochib. World news was outdated by the time I heard it.

Since Yochib was at an altitude of over 5,000 feet, the weather was often too cold for comfort. A hard cold rain would fall pitilessly for days on end. The Indians at least had a place for a fire in the center of their huts and could huddle there to keep warm. I had no such luxury. My Coleman lantern gave out what heat I could muster. With the shutters on my windows closed in the rainy season, it was very dark and confining in that little house.

Vital equipment broke down. The generators in my Coleman lantern and in my stove would become clogged with the sediment in the white gasoline I used for fuel even though I had carefully filtered it.

Dating from childhood, I had always been susceptible to bronchial illness. I learned to dress in layers, sweater upon sweater.

Because their only source of water was the river far below, the Indians used very little water on themselves or their clothes.

Worst of all was accepting the hospitality of their food. With my finicky stomach, I barely managed to eat their unhygienic offerings but, as a guest, I dared not offend them.

There would have been no reason for me to stay in that strange unwelcoming setting, but for this:

The love of Christ constraineth me.
II Cor. 5:14

And His love did fill me as I tried to identify with my Tzeltal neighbors. One by one, I learned to love them as individuals. It was a love that could have only come from the Lord Himself.

The dark places of the earth
are full of the habitations of cruelty.
Psalm 74:20

Something was wrong.

I glanced at Maria
who stood trambling in my doorway.

Her blanched face
was frozen in terror.

Chapter Four

Maria

"Maria! What happened?"

"Nichu's wife! I passed her on the trail!"

Puzzled, I led my Indian friend inside the house. Her steps faltered. She was truly sick.

"But what...?" My questions dropped off. I had been in Yochib long enough to realize Western ideas of "cause and effect" had little bearing on life in a Tzeltal setting.

Nichu was a *shaman* (witch doctor). That was reason enough for Maria to develop a raging fever from a chance encounter with his wife. Nichu had power of life or death over Maria. He could cast a curse of sickness on her. He could "eat her soul", or that of her little girl, if he so chose. For a few bottles of liquor, he could give her to any man who wanted her. Maria was literally bound in fear to this old man. She provided for me glimpses into the unrelieved darkness of the Oxchuc Tzeltals.

When I had first come to Yochib and rented my little house from Villa, Maria had been part of the bargain. She and her four-year-old daughter, Maruch, kept me company the many weeks I was without a partner. They were the bridge between me and their world for Maria was my source of information for anything I wanted to know, from the proper price of eggs to her people's customs.

Fine-featured and highly intelligent, Maria had been deserted by her husband, a *shaman* who had fled to the coast after killing another Indian. Since then, Maria and Maruch had lived in a cornstalk hut barely large enough for the two of them to get inside. She had no man to help her construct a more suitable dwelling and that was all she could manage herself. They shared this tiny hovel with a setting hen and Maria's few clay pots in one corner.

In a nearby thatch lean-to lay the graves of Maria's first husband and four other children. On the Day of the Dead, Maria carefully provided food for their spirits by placing orange halves and specially prepared dishes on their graves. She then spent a long time wailing over their departed souls.

With little Maruch bundled on her back in a coarse carrying cloth, Maria came frequently to help me. Whether or not I ever learned her language was a matter of complete indifference to her. But she humored me with the repetition of words or phrases until she became bored with the process. Sometimes, when a *shaman* whose power she dreaded came along the path, Maria would abruptly stop and leave my house. If a neighbor with an evil tongue passed by my open door, she would make some hasty excuse and bundle little Maruch up and head toward home.

Though she was a very poor language informant, Maria served another useful purpose. She carried water for me from the river in large clay pots too heavy for me even to lift, let alone carry for a half hour up a steep mountainous trail. With the tumpline across her forehead and her back bent forward in tremendous strain, Maria was a true representation of the burdened Indian with little relief from her grievous load.

I had to be extremely cautious about my use of water. Dishes were scalded in boiling water but this water was saved to use again, possibly to wash vegetables for the next meal.

There was no such luxury as a shower or tub bath. I sponged from a basin. Sometimes mail was six weeks in coming.

A succession of companions for a few weeks or months at a time relieved my loneliness. But these young women had assignments to other tribes and did not become deeply involved in the Tzeltal work.

In all the area around, there was no medical help other than the *shamans*. Because my little house was only a few hundred yards from the main trail, many Indians accustomed to visiting the Villas came to me for assistance with their physical ailments. I had never been trained in medicine but I found myself doctoring their ills as best I could. Gnawing tropical ulcers, eyes running from infection, children pot-bellied from parasites, dysentery, *machete* wounds following a drunken fight; their need was great and my resources were small.

I also found my time very limited for language learning. It required great discipline not to get "bogged down" with the daily routine of just maintaining life in Yochib.

With whatever partner I had at the time, I would set out to visit the huts of our Indian neighbors up and down the mountainside. In order not to startle the residents by the sudden appearance of foreigners (and to give them time to restrain their vicious dogs), we learned to call out, "I have come to see you."

Even though the highland Tzeltal was different from the dialect we had been studying in the low country, we were able to make ourselves understood. Our use of their language disarmed the Indian women we found at home.

We would be offered a low wooden seat and then we would watch as our hostess continued with her day's activities. Sometimes she would be deftly coiling strips of clay to make a clay pot. All the while, a running conversation kept up. Our language file was growing.

Even when it was obvious, we would ask, "What are you doing?"

She would laugh and supply the answer, pleased that we took such an interest in her daily life.

She might laugh at our clumsy efforts to weave or to shape *tortillas*. But we were learning the language and we were making friends! Their amusement at our interest in their mundane affairs served as a bridge to our acceptance in Yochib.

We began to get a glimpse of the intricacies of family structure among the Tzeltals. There were obligations of kinship and there were marriage taboos. Land ownership was governed by lineal descent. A web of kinship ties interlaced the entire community of over five thousand Oxchuc Indians.

The implications of this tightly-knit social group became increasingly clear to me; a deviation from the norm of tribal custom would be subject to stiff social pressure from others of the tribe. However, if one of the group accepted "the good new words" translated into Tzeltal, he would have an advantage no outsider would ever have to use his social network to communicate God's Word to his extended family.

Several weeks after our arrival in Yochib, we were visited by our neighbor, Alonzo Tomato. In knee-length, white cotton garb banded by gaudy orange and red embroidery on each sleeve, Alonzo was characterized by a self-confidence not usually evident in our Indian friends. With the help of a large flannel-backed board and some colored cut-out figures, I related the Death and Resurrection of Jesus. Alonzo listened with such attentiveness his eyes barely blinked. I told him the meaning of a savior, "One who habitually helps."

He sighed in reluctance as I folded up the flannelgraph board.

"Too bad my relatives can't see this, too," he remarked with regret.

My heart racing at this obvious opening by the Lord, I assured him, "Oh, we'll do it all over again tomorrow, if they come."

The next afternoon, others began to arrive until there were seven in all. The afternoon of the third telling, eight more came to hear this "old, old story" completely new to them. By this time Alonzo knew the story well enough so that he could tell it in Tzeltal himself, not missing a single detail.

Suddenly, in the midst of Alonzo's recital, in walked Juan Nich. Juan was a budding *shaman* and he had already indicated his hostility to us and to our message. His manner toward us had always been cynical and there was an expression of cruelty about his mouth. I held my breath. It would not be unlike him to disrupt with some uncouth remark. I sent a swift silent prayer upward.

Juan looked about him, seeming to note each person in the group by name. Then he sat down, and listened as docilely as the rest!

My partners were extremely helpful in preparing some of the earliest primers for these people as we emphasized the necessity of learning to read in order to have God's Word for themselves. They were a pre-literate people and they had no idea words could be written on paper to convey meaning in the Tzeltal language. We used the Laubach chart with vowels to which the corresponding consonants could be added to form syllables. Katherine Voigtlander, a dedicated artist, illustrated these simple booklets with drawings suitable to the environment of the people. Elaine Mielke (later married to Uncle Cam) invented all sorts of reading games to make the venture an exciting one for our people. Step by step, we were laying the groundwork for the future.

As often as four times a day, we would bring out the flannelgraph and tell the story of Jesus to different groups. From their mountain village up the trail came wild Cancuc Tzeltals with their hair as matted as a thatch roof. Tenejapa men, garbed in their black wool garments, leaned on their staffs, listening attentively. Shy, long-legged men from Tenango stopped in on their way to market to purchase fire-rockets and candles for the coming *fiesta*. A throng of schoolboys raced over from school each afternoon to learn the newest Tzeltal Bible verse or the latest chorus we had translated. The Indians had never learned to sing anything but raucous drinking chants but now they were singing the wonders of our Lord. We had asked God to "*bring many sons unto His glory*," and now these were beginning to show evidence that they, too, belonged to His family!

The entrance of Thy word giveth light.
Psalm 119:130

He stood apart from the rest,
shifting his market produce
from one hand to the other.

Lanky, in a handwoven garment
and red sash,
he seemed the typical Indian
on his way to market.

His manner was dejected;
I sensed he had been only half-listening
as I told the flannelgraph story
to a little group outside my house.

I hadn't noticed this man before.

He lingered
long enough for me to approach him.

Chapter Five

Martin

"Did God's words arrive in your heart?" I asked.

He shook his head slowly. "No, not a word arrived in my heart."

"If you come back again and listen, then, little by little, God's words will arrive in your heart," I promised.

I bought a prickly *chayote* and some string beans from him and learned his name, Martin Gourd.

Martin turned away, his shoulders drooping. Everything about this man emanated sorrow. He was not an old man but his bearing was so dejected that he seemed aged.

He did return a second and a third time. And he told me his story as he began to feel confidence in my concern for him.

"My first wife died when she was very young. Someone, maybe the *shaman*, had put a curse on her. I lighted thirteen candles on the altar in my house. And I knelt before the wooden cross and prayed to it to save her.

"Then my only brother got sick. I carried him on my back to many *shamans*. I paid them many bottles of liquor to save his life. They took his pulse and then they beat me to lift the curse from my brother. He died last week."

Tears welled up in my eyes as I listened to him. He was deep in grief and despair. And he was one of thousands held under the bondage of the *shamans.*

Through all the years I was in Mexico, the struggle against the power of the *shaman* was ever present. The *shamans* terrorized the people with their curses. They also held in their hands the power of life and death. When anyone became ill, the family carried him to the *shaman.* It was necessary to pay him with a great deal of liquor because inebriation was a necessary adjunct to dealing with "sacred things." When the *shaman* was drunk enough to begin his ritual of "healing," he would put both thumbs on the wrist of the prone patient. Though actually the pulse he felt was his own, he then claimed he could discern who had cast the spell of sickness on the patient.

He might ask, "Did you not show respect to your mother-in-law?"

"Did you offend one of your relatives?"

"Did you trespass on somebody's land rights?"

The infraction could be very minor from the Western viewpoint but any violation of social taboos or kinship system would be cause enough for retribution or fear of retribution. They did indeed fear "fear itself." Incomprehensible to us was the pall of superstition that dominated their lives.

Even owning some small item more than their neighbor could be a cause for a curse. Everyone had a thatched roof on his house. Even if some industrious Indian could afford a tin one, he dared not put it on for fear of a jealous neighbor casting a curse on him. If one man managed to purchase a pair of shoes, he might be subject to a curse because he thought he was "better" than his fellows.

The *shamans* were accorded a place of reverential fear among the Tzeltals. Casting a spell of evil was the reverse function of healing. The man who could cure disease was obviously able to cause it.

Martin was weary of their power over him. Perhaps this, more than the realization of Christ's forgiveness of his sins, drew him to the flannelgraph stories. Little by little, I was able to show him that God did not want him to live in fear for "perfect love casteth out fear." And no love could be more perfect than Christ's love!

As God's Word slowly "arrived in his heart," I wanted to teach Martin to read for then he would be able to learn from the Bible and not be dependent on oral teaching. For one who had never even held a book in his hands, learning to "see paper" was a time-consuming task. Between his reading lessons, Martin would forget what he had learned from the time before. The expression he used was, "I have lost it out of my heart."

It slowly dawned on me that if I could combine this expression with the Indian word for "sin," I would find a much-needed word for the Gospel of Mark I was translating. When Martin came for his next reading session, I tried the newly-coined expression on him,

"Martin, when we believe on the Lord Jesus, God 'loses all of our sins out of His heart.'"

His face lighted up instantly with comprehension.

"Is that what God does with our sins when we believe?" he asked. I had found the expression I needed for "forgive!" As I worked more and more on the Tzeltal language, I realized that it was perfectly adequate to convey every spiritual idea. My task as a translator was to marshal every resource to find the words to impart to the Indians what Scripture says.

Martin was much better at memorizing than at reading. I had written a number of hymns in Tzeltal because I realized that the constant repetition of assurance was what these people needed. Martin invariably personalized these hymns.

"Jesus can save you" became "Jesus can save me." I knew then that Martin knew the Lord. His whole manner changed. From a despondent, dejected man, he became full of life and energy. His steps bounded with vitality. He came often to my house although he lived an hour and a quarter away, up a steep mountainside.

He began to bring his family to hear. His aged father could barely make it down the mountainside with his staff. He listened intently, an astounded expression on his face.

"You mean the sun is not alive?"

The Oxchuc Tzeltals had believed that the sun was God and that the images in the Oxchuc church were the means to a somewhat dubious salvation. The most amazing fact of all the old man repeated over and over:

"Jesus bore our sins!"

When Martin explained to his father that "God knows how to write" and that He would write his name in the Book of Life in heaven, the old man nodded his head in assent. He did want his name included!

But Maria, Martin's sweet-faced wife, was not interested in changing from the old ways to those of God. Martin confessed to me that he had hit her for not wanting to believe as he did!

One day Martin came to accompany me up the hour-and-a-quarter climb to his hut perched high up a steep rocky mountainside. He carried my flannelgraph and accordion on his back. His little hut had been neatly swept for our visit. Like most Indian huts, the thatch was smoke-blackened. The walls of upright planks had been tied in place with pliable vines.

Martin had gathered his family and neighbors together to hear what God's Book said. He wanted their hearts to be changed as his had been. This was the beginning of a concern for the salvation of others that was to take Martin all over the Oxchuc region, preaching the Christ who had "lost his sins out of His heart."

Martin was the only believer for some time. When market day approached, we prayed constantly for strength for him to overcome the tremendous temptation of liquor urged on him by those who could not tolerate the fact that he no longer was one with them in riotous living. We knew how frail is man and Martin came from a culture where drinking was part of life.

Though he never became a fluent reader, Martin was extremely helpful as a language informant. He gave me the data I needed in order to meet Wycliffe's standards of grammar analysis before I could successfully translate the New Testament in Tzeltal. An article of mine was published in the April, 1948, International Journal of American Linguistics (vol. XIV, No. 2), entitled "Tzeltal (Mayan) Noun and Verb Morphology."

Martin gained a reverence for his own language as he began to see God's Word in Tzeltal.

"We must do it well so it will be just the way we talk and do it carefully because it is God's Word," he would say.

I took special delight in the idioms of the language. To be "of one heart" meant to be wholehearted. To have "two hearts" meant to be undecided or vacillating. To have "a straight heart" meant to be just, as God is just. To have a "standing-up heart" meant to be enthusiastic. To have a "sitting-down heart" meant to be at peace.

Many of these idioms found their way into the pages of the New Testament. I wrote home:

Hearing not a word but pure Tzeltal, I am beginning even to think in the language. I hope to concentrate on revision of the rest of Mark from now on, to have it ready to check with Dr. Nida of the American Bible Society when he comes to Chiapas in May.

Martin was a source for explaining the mystic beliefs of these descendants of the ancient Mayans. It was necessary for me to grasp these concepts of their religious beliefs in order to avoid certain references to God which could have been confused with their old pagan ideas.

Almost every culture has a version of the "Flood" story. Martin, a gifted story teller, passed on to me the Tzeltal account.

"The world is flat. Four pillars hold it up at each corner, to one of which the Antichrist is chained. His struggles to free himself in order to destroy humanity is what causes earthquakes. The sky arches overhead like an upside-down *posol* (corn gruel) bowl. The navel of the world is Oxchuc. A 'very black God' is angry at the inhabitants of the world because they cause such a stench to rise to heaven. He plans to send a flood at any moment to destroy us all. But St. Thomas from his niche in the Oxchuc church, sends mules laden with firerockets up to heaven to appease the Angry One so that we can survive. A cross standing at the edge of the world where floodwaters lap the shore prevents the disaster that mankind deserves."

The story gave me tremendous insight into their cosmology. It was a complete syncretism of pagan and Catholic beliefs. I realized then that it would be confusing to them to talk about "God in heaven" for they would mentally equate Him with the Sun of their legends or with the "Angry One" of their Catholic beliefs.

In this narrative, Martin had also given me the word for "salvation." The Tzeltal word means, "To survive, escape, get saved, become free, to get well, to get out of jail." By using this term in the context of Scripture some Tzeltals began to realize what "salvation" meant. It became a part of the vocabulary of the New Testament.

In a letter to my family I wrote,

It certainly is a burden upon my heart to give out the Word here knowing that it is a matter of life and death to those who hear. It either blots out their guilt if they believe or it deepens their guilt if they don't believe. If we were looking at circumstances instead of looking to the Lord, the darkness here would seem impenetrable.

From almost the first day, Juan Nich became our outspoken adversary. He lived a short distance below our little house on the Yochib mountainside. He was a budding *shaman* and he held tremendous influence over the people around. And he hated the Gospel.

He was a cruel man. Many times his sweet little second wife, Rosalia, would take refuge in our house from his angry beatings. This did not increase his love for us.

One time, as I was working at my little table just under the window, in strode drunken Juan Nich with a gun slung over his shoulder, angry words pouring in a torrent from his mouth. He glared about my small house as if he would like to consume it in fury. I was frightened but God did not allow my fear to be evident. I spoke gently to my intruder and he grunted a drunken oath and departed.

But his special hatred was reserved for Martin. Whenever he had opportunity, he sneered at Martin's faith and at his refusal to become drunk on market days. One day, word reached Martin that Juan Nich was coming that night to shoot him. Perhaps realizing that Juan Nich could kill him in ambush if he did attempt escape, Martin refused to leave his home. Instead, he sat in his hut all night playing his victrola with his little red hymnal open before him, determined that if he were to be killed, he would die giving out the Gospel. The bullets never came. Martin had learned that God did, indeed, give His angels charge over him.

Gospel Recordings, founded by Joy Ridderhof about the time Uncle Cam was starting Wycliffe Bible Translators, had made six records in lowland Tzeltal for use among our people. Though the dialect was different, the message could be understood by the highlanders. For an illiterate population, these recordings provided a way to sow the seed, for villagers would gather around their "talking box" and listen over and over to the words of salvation. And the records also created an appetite for learning to read that the people themselves might know how to learn more of God's message to them.

Daily, I brought out my hand-wound victrola and played the Tzeltal records of the Prodigal Son or Christ's Death and Resurrection or other messages which revealed God's love for us. Sometimes my audience would be several Indian women sitting on the ground nursing their babies. Often, one or two of the *shamans*, their eyes dull from too much liquor over too many years, joined us. Women struggling up the mountain from the river below with heavy jugs of water found my yard a welcome respite. Men on their way to or from Las Casas often stopped to listen for a few minutes and stayed to ask questions.

"None of our idols can save us?"

"God loves us and wants to save us? His heart is good!"

"What can we give God? Candles, incense?"

"You mean the sun and moon aren't gods? What is the name of the One Who made them?"

Martin became enthralled with the possibilities of these recordings. On his own initiative, he strapped the victrola to his back and began visiting the Oxchuc Tzeltals for miles around with this new message.

"This is God's Word! And the songs are in 'the real language,' too! This is good to put into our hearts, good to believe!"

It was good. We had been working with the Tzeltals for a long time and now we were beginning to see the seeds planted in hardship, loneliness and trial begin to bear fruit.

Ye have need of patience that,
after ye have done the will of God,
ye might receive the promise.
                                   Hebrews 10:36

"A place of entering in" -
that was the actual meaning of the word,

Yochib.

It wasn't truly a town
so much as a crossroads of trails
leading either up and down the mountain
or to and from Las Casas.

The name refers to an immense cave
at the foot of the mountain
where the shallow river
from which the Tzeltals drew their water
disappeared underground.

Chapter Six

Yochib

Near the mouth of the cave, three crosses marked the site of the weekly bush-market, a place where Tzeltals from three major highland dialects carried on a brisk barter.

To us, Yochib became the place of "entering in" to a fuller comprehension of the hopelessness of those who had never had the light of the knowledge of God or seen His love in the face of Jesus.

It was also an "entering in" to a life of trust from day to day, almost minute to minute, for even the safety of our lives.

Every market day ended the same way with many jugs of sugar-cane liquor consumed. Fighting would break out over the most trivial of incidents. And someone (or two or three) would be left wounded or dying from *machete* slashings.

Our welcome in Yochib was, at best, tenuous. The schoolteacher and his wife who had at first been friendly, turned cold when they realized we were teaching the Bible. As the *shamans* realized the Gospel posed a real challenge to their power over the people, they became more hostile. There were drunken threats to burn down the little house I lived in.

Juan Nich, especially, never ceased to undermine the ministry and my security. And yet, when he was sick, he came to me for medicine!

Professor Villa had loaned me his house for six months. When the time was nearly up, he advised me to leave, at least for the time being.

"There is great persecution of Protestants," he warned. The repercussions might reach even to remote Chiapas.

While my interim partners and I had been concentrating on life in Yochib, in Mexico City pickets were parading before all the Protestant-owned stores to keep them from prospering. Attempts had been made on the life of Christian workers there and some believers had been killed. Services were interrupted by gas bombs. Newspaper articles and cartoons depicting foreigners "strangling Indians" with the Word of God had fueled fires of opposition.

In spite of the warnings, I was extremely reluctant to leave. After all the years of trying to gain a foothold among the Tzeltals, I felt I had barely started. There were a few new believers. They had no Word of God in their own language on which to feed if I were to leave. Most of what they knew had been committed to memory through the use of the flannelgraph stories. It was a terribly heartbreaking decision to make but there seemed no alternative.

Uncle Cam was in the process of initiating the first Jungle Camp for Wycliffe trainees and he asked me to be one of the vanguard. Located in lowland Tzeltal territory, it was a three-day journey on horseback out of the mountains. But at least, I would still be among the people God had called me to. Shortly before Christmas, our little band started out. There were tears among the Indians I was leaving and there were tears on my part. Once again, I was a "pilgrim."

And once again, the Lord revealed that "*His way is perfect.*" I had been lonely at times in Yochib. This Christmas, there were nine of us translators to celebrate together with a pine tree, small gifts and best of all, the joy of singing the familiar Christmas carols.

For two nights in a row, I presented for the first time to the Indians at the ranch where we were staying, the story of Jesus and His birth. I used the flannelgraph, well-worn by this time, and the accordion to accompany the hymns I had previously translated for the highland Tzeltals. I was reminded again that when one door closes, the Lord will open another. His Word was brought to a part of the Tzeltal tribe which had never heard.

Along the banks of the Santa Cruz River were three huts of typical mud walls and thatched roofs. Here we hung our hammocks and called ourselves "at home." Jungle Camp was designed by Uncle Cam to train new translators heading for the jungle tribes of Peru. Situated at the very edge of the pine forest there, we heard reports of alligators in the river, deer in the forest and even a jaguar venturing into an Indian neighbor's yard to eat his chickens!

Living conditions were primitive in the extreme and served to teach new missionaries how to cope with the hardest circumstances. They swam in the river, learned to canoe, discovered which foods were edible and which poisonous, learned how to handle a *machete* and build a shelter from the bushes about them and they learned how to deal with loneliness and isolation.

Survival techniques, as well as learning to communicate in Tzeltal, were part of the rigorous schedule. Because of their contact with the surrounding Tzeltal Indians, many of the trainees departing Jungle Camp continued to pray for these they had learned to love.

We were forty miles overland from the nearest town and there was no food available except what we could purchase from our closest Indian neighbors. Just ten minutes' walk down the trail lived Doroteo and his large family. By fording the river, more than knee-deep in places, we were able to reach a whole colony of Tzeltal huts, about forty in all, clustered neatly together on a hillside.

There had been a recent revenge killing of an Indian in that village by a posse of whites. The Indians were understandably filled with hostility and fear of any other white person. Two of the young missionary men insisted on accompanying Esther Matteson and me when we went to try to buy some food in the village. They carried guns on their shoulders. We felt that was a foolhardy way to enter a village and urged them to wait a long way from the main path instead of coming along with us.

We came into the clearing around the village and there was not a soul in evidence. Every door was shuttered tight. But there was the obvious presence of humanity breathing behind those tight-closed doors.

In Tzeltal, I called out, "Have you any eggs to sell? Any beans? Any *chayotes*?"

No answer, but Esther and I persisted in our greetings, smiling and calling out in Tzeltal. Eventually, a door cracked open. One curious woman had ventured to look at us. Behind her trembled her fearful husband certain that he was to face death! Then, down the row of huts, came the unmistakable sound of the death wail - the keening of the widow who had lost her husband in the recent posse killing. We knew we dared not linger, for fear of causing another tragedy. We did stay long enough to tell them that we would buy whatever they had to sell over at our Jungle Camp. Gradually, the fear disappeared from their eyes. Little children slipped cautiously out of their homes and reached out to touch the skirts of these strange-looking white women!

That began our entrance into the trust of these Tzeltals of the lowlands. None of them had ever heard, even once, of Jesus' power to save. Often they came to Jungle Camp with their produce and often they stayed to listen to the flannelgraph stories. The old man of the village, said to be a *shaman*, came to hear, bringing his family. His name was Lazaro. His eyes never left my face as I told the Bible story of Lazarus. It was seed well sown.

Of them all, Doroteo proved to be our chief joy.

"My heart likes God's Word," he explained simply.

Without any instigation on my part, he decided not to participate in the traditional religious rituals.

The old grandmother who lived next to Doroteo became a true believer.

"No one ever came to tell me before," she said. "Maybe now, even though I am old, a word or two will stay in my heart."

For over two years, I tried desperately to get permission to return to Yochib on a permanent basis. I did manage to spend intermittent weeks there but never officially. And yet, because of this "uprootedness", a vast area of lowland Tzeltals were contacted and the seed sown to be harvested in later years.

Nothing happens "by chance" in God's plan. How many times I have seen a "chance" encounter, a "chance" meeting, a "chance" conversation work out to the fulfillment of His overall plan for His people.

On one of my trips from Las Casas, I "happened" to be riding on a bus filled with *mestizos* and an occasional Indian. Stops for flat tires were frequent. One time when all the passengers disembarked for the driver to change the tire, I struck up a conversation with a *mestizo* who was obviously well-educated. He turned out to be the Head of Indian Affairs for Chiapas and a true advocate for the Indians. His name was don Manuel Castellanos.

Some time later, when in Las Casas, I "happened" to meet Giles Healy, a Carnegie photographer for the United Fruit Company. He had recently made a rare archaeological find, Bonampak, an ancient Mayan site, and I had always been keenly interested in Mayan history and archaeology. It also "happened" that this same don Manuel whom I had met on the bus many months previous, was also visiting Mr. Healy. We remembered each other, of course. American women working with Indians were not a common occurrence in Mexico!

"And how is the work among the modern Maya coming at Yochib?" he asked.

"It would be a lot better if I could obtain permission to stay there," I explained with a rueful laugh.

Don Manuel was at once solicitous. He heard my story, then immediately offered a solution. He, as head of Indian Affairs, would take a hand in it.

First, he met with the schoolteacher when he came to Las Casas. A few weeks later, he took a full day's trip on horseback out to Yochib and met with the local Indian officials to plead my case. Perhaps it was because of his prestigious position that they eventually came to an agreement. I was to receive permission to live in Villa's house for three more years.

His heart is in the hand of the Lord,
and he turneth it whithersoever he wills.
Proverbs 21:1

Domineering Isidro Ensin, town president of Oxchuc, gripped his silver-tipped staff in one hand and a borrowed pen in the other. The staff was a symbol of authority and the pen a sign of education. Almost as if it were his idea in the first place, he affixed his signature with a flourish to the rental document. Andrew Badger, the surly *shaman* on whose land Villa's house stood, added his thumbprint and grudgingly accepted the one hundred *pesos* rent money.

I could hardly believe it! After all this time, I was once again "officially" a resident of Yochib!

I was anxious to complete my work on the Tzeltal New Testament. There was no hope of the Tzeltal believers ever being able to grow spiritually without the Word of God in their own language. Martin was faithful in helping and diligent to get the words into the idiom of the Tzeltals. Since the Tzeltals were not a literate people, it was also necessary to prepare primers for them to learn on a beginning level.

They did, however, have one book from ancient times they highly revered. The first thirteen days of every year it was transferred from one group of Indian officials to another with special rites.

Carefully guarded, the book was brought from its resting-place, put on a table with thirteen candles, thirteen rosaries, thirteen gourds of tobacco and thirteen bowls of corn gruel. Then the Indian officials would kneel before it. They burned incense, shot off fire-rockets and called the book, "Our Lord." At the end of thirteen days, the book was solemnly escorted to a hut on the outskirts of town, where it was kept under guard all year long.

All that the book contained was twelve paper sheets, nine with writing on both sides, orders given by Spanish authorities in the year 1674! I wanted to give them The Book handed down by Divine Authority.

Most of the inhabitants of the surrounding area were delighted to have me back in Yochib for I had made many friends. A steady stream of callers found their way to my door. Increasingly, I found my limited knowledge of medicine drained to the utmost. I was not a nurse yet the pitiful plight of Indian children with their stomachs swollen from worms, the festering wounds on men from a *machete* slashing, the deep cough of pneumonia wracking the bodies of frail babies, the endless spitting which accompanies tuberculosis almost crushed me when added to the spiritual needs.

I did the best I could. I had no microscope to diagnose illness but I prescribed worm medicine by the case. I cleaned the *machete* wounds with hydrogen peroxide and bandaged them with sulfa powder. I tried to teach the mothers the simple rudiments of hygiene. Because water was such a scarcity and soap was non-existent, they could not grasp the importance of cleanliness. They mixed their corn gruel with unwashed hands and drank from a common family bowl. Implements were never washed, let alone scalded to kill germs.

When I sent medicine home for continuous treatment of illness, I could never be certain it would be taken properly. Either the patient would assume that "if one pill is good, then five must be better" and take them all at once or he might decide that "one didn't do him any good" so he would refuse to take the others and not get the medicine into his system. It seemed a losing battle.

But as some of the Tzeltals found that the medicine dispensed by me worked better than the pulse-taking of the *shamans*, more and more found their way to my door often after long arduous journeys being carried on a relative's back. How could I refuse to help them?

Language work was frustratingly slow. Interruptions filled my day. I tried to work on the language after I had shut the door at night. I was overwhelmed by the magnitude of the task, by the medical work because I was not trained for it and in analyzing this Mayan language because there were not sufficient hours in the day to concentrate on it.

Most of all I needed a partner - one who would share my burden and love for the Tzeltals. My father made his prayer request to the Lord very specific: a permanent partner for Marianna, one who was a nurse.

Shall the prey be taken from the mighty,
or the lawful captive delivered?
                                         Isaiah 49:24

Christmas Day came and went.

It was very different
from our traditional celebration
with family and friends
with a decorated tree
and splendidly-wrapped gifts.

I heard no cheery holiday greetings
and saw no familiar faces from home.

New Year's Day was even lonelier.

Faced with the prospect or another year,
I wondered what future it held
for my goal
of giving the Word of God
to these unresponsive hearts.

Chapter Seven

Florence, R.N.

January 2, 1947. I was just getting ready to eat another lonely evening meal when I heard voices outside the door and the sound of a horse's snorts. Before my caller could knock, I opened the door.

"Hello, Marianna," she said with a tired smile as she dismounted. She was dressed in a heavy sweater and full skirt and her fair skin was ruddy from the cold mountain air.

"Remember me? I'm Florence Gerdel."

Of course I remembered her! We had met briefly in Mexico City a few months before. I helped her inside my little house and offered her some supper. While we ate, she explained,

"The Director sent me out to be with you, at least temporarily."

It was Florence's first visit to Tzeltal country, her first visit to Yochib, her first assignment to missionary work. She felt she had been well initiated that day for she had come ten hours on horseback to this lonely outpost with no company but one pack animal and a guide. She spoke no Spanish at all!

There was little doubt in my mind Who had sent her. Just about the time my own strength was sapped to the point of utter weariness, Florence came to be part of my life.

Florence began her nursing career in Yochib with no time to rest, become acclimated or acculturated. The patients needing her skills were at the door early next morning and they never stopped coming. She saw gunshot wounds, chronic eye inflammations, malaria and worm-infested children. Her excellent training and natural loving concern overcame the barrier of the lack of a common language between them.

Florence and I were almost identical in size and build but my hair was light brown, hers was pure spun gold. Since none of the Indians had ever seen hair of such color, they assumed Florence was my mother! We laughed about that because she was actually three-and-a-half years younger than I.

Florence's presence in Yochib created a whole new climate for me. I had had no one there to share amusing incidents or outlooks. I sometimes went for weeks without hearing English. And most of all, I had needed someone to pray with. The burdens of these blinded, hurting people were almost more than one person could bear alone. I had needed Florence and so did the Tzeltals. The Lord had sent her.

Florence was quickly introduced into the birth customs of the highland Tzeltals for less than a month after she arrived in Yochib, she was summoned to assist in a difficult case. In an account published in "The American Anthropologist" (Volume 51, No. 1, 1949, pp. 158-159) she wrote,

One afternoon a highland Tzeltal girl came to our house asking for some panela, a molded lump of native brown sugar, explaining that she wanted it for a friend who was about to give birth to her third child. Within two hours, she returned with an urgent request for my colleague and myself to go to the parturient because she was going to die. She evidently expected us to be able to save her. Since the term in this dialect of Tzeltal may signify either "to be sick" or "to die", we questioned her for more details. We learned that a baby girl had been born but that the afterbirth which is normally delivered in fifteen to forty-five minutes, had not appeared. Although we knew this to be an unusual but not fatal occurrence, we followed our insistent guide up the steep, muddy trail until we reached a native house.

Inside, there were many relatives and friends seated about the fire in the center of the hard-packed dirt floor. The new mother was kneeling on the ground, pushing downward on her uterus with all of her strength. Others had assisted till they were fatigued. Beside her sat her mother-in-law on a low wooden block holding the newborn child. She alternately wept and moaned, exclaiming first that the baby was going to die and then that the mother, too, was going to die.

The mother-in-law continually begged us to help. Having nothing more suitable, we gave the patient one and a half tablets of aspirin.

After nearly two more hours had elapsed, the assistance of a witch-doctor was sought to discover who had cast a curse upon the unfortunate mother. After the customary greetings, he felt the patient's pulse in the usual manner. After a long discussion, they successfully "revealed" who had cast a curse upon the mother. She confessed that the man named was the one. Suddenly the placenta descended intact.

In order to make certain that this new-born girl-child would develop into a capable woman, a weaving batten was placed under her right arm, a spindle in her right hand, and a stone for grinding corn beside her. With this brief ceremony, the tension and uncertainty of the day was relieved.

Every day brought fresh challenges to Florence. There was a young girl who had been bitten by a snake five days before! Her parents had been carrying her around to various *shamans* to see if they could reverse the curse. When Florence asked if they had cut the skin to suck out the poison, they said they had not because the seven-year-old child did not want them to. Her whole leg and foot were swollen tremendously. However, with Florence's kindly manner, they felt encouraged enough to bring the child faithfully for treatment. Within a week, the swelling had gone down and she lived.

Every market day brought the wounded who had been in drinking quarrels. One man "died three times" from loss of blood due to a deep gash in his temple. A rainy day invariably brought people complaining of coughs. Youngsters suffering from all sorts of intestinal parasites were carried to our door. We had a limited supply of medicine to treat an unlimited number of patients and the nearest source of medical supplies was a day away by horseback.

As much as anything, Florence discovered the Tzeltals needed instruction in sanitary methods. When mothers brought their little ones to her with sores all over, she showed them how to bathe the children even providing the soap. But then the clothes were dirty and laundry facilities were totally unthought of!

Even more difficult for her were the vague complaints like "everything becomes black" or "wind in my muscles." At Mt. Zion Hospital in San Francisco where she had taken her training, she had not had to treat cases like these!

She had been with me only six weeks when word came that Uncle Cam and his wife, Elaine, and new baby, Grace, had been in an airplane crash

at Jungle Camp. Since geographically, Florence
was the closest nurse to the site of the tragedy,
she was summoned to go minister to the
Townsends who had been severely injured. She
traveled three days to the lowlands with only an
Indian guide for company. When the Townsends
were well enough to be flown out to Mexico City
for care, the Director asked her to go even farther
to the Lacandon tribe where a translator's wife was
very ill. On this trip, the young Wycliffe man who
was accompanying Florence somehow became
separated from her along the trail and she had to
spend the night with nothing but the jungle for a
floor and the Indian guide for protection. Since
snakes were in abundance in this area, her true
protection came directly from above.

I lay down and slept;
I awoke, for the Lord sustained me.

Psalm 3:5

It was the day before Easter when she returned
to Yochib. I had been alone for five weeks. How I
welcomed her back!

The medical work continued without break; if
anything, it increased as word spread among the
Indians that "Lorensa" helped more than the
pulse-takers with various types of illness. But
very few of our patients could be trusted to follow
directions if they left Florence's supervising eye.

Many times it was critical that a small infant be
watched throughout the night or he would not
have survived. We decided to clear out the small
addition Villa had built for his students and turn
it into a dispensary for the more serious patients.
This greatly increased our responsibilities to the
people for we seldom had any time by ourselves

but it was the means of keeping a number from dying.

Still, there were the heartbreaks of too little, too late. Many came to Florence only as a last resort; they had visited *shaman* after *shaman* for healing and came only when the patient was literally breathing his last. Especially when we saw that the illness was of a nature that might have been alleviated if we could have treated it in time, we felt genuine anguish. We never became thoroughly accustomed to this kind of grief.

Even those who had accepted the Lord sometimes reverted to their old ways in the face of calamity. Since they believed everything was due to a curse, it was only natural that they would seek the assistance of the native pulse-takers who specialized in curses and the lifting of them.

We had never been told life among the Tzeltals would be easy. Yet, when the darkness of Satan persisted so steadily in those who heard but could not perceive, we found ourselves discouraged. How long until they believed firmly enough to allow their hearts to be changed?

Even the captives of the mighty
shall be taken away,
and the prey of the terrible shall be delivered.
Isaiah 49:25

"Who made this book?"

The query came from a young Tzeltal man
as he turned a small mimeographed booklet
of thirty-five hymns in his hand.

He had not known there was such a thing,
a book with Tzeltal words written in it.

He had been in school for three months
when he was a child
but he thought all the words in the world
were printed in Spanish.

Chapter Eight

Juan Mucha

Martin Gourd, uncertain tutor as he was, explained. Two *gringas* (foreign women) who lived beyond them on the mountainside possessed a copy of "God's Book." Martin had seen the Book and had even helped translate some of it into "the real language."

Juan Mucha was fascinated. He plied Martin with questions.

"What would these *gringas* say if I showed up at their house and asked them to tell me more about God?"

"They would welcome you," Martin assured him.

"Should I approach them with lighted candles? Or with offerings of flowers?"

"No. Just go up to them and say,'I have come, *me'tik*'. They understand the 'real language.'"

It was nearly dawn and Martin had spent the night with the extended Mucha family of Corralito, playing his beloved victrola with its Gospel records.

The afternoon before had been an exciting one for Martin. In the town square of Abasolo where a *fiesta* was in full swing, he had cranked up his victrola and begun to play the message in clear, loud Tzeltal.

The priest, suddenly aware that more Indians were gathering about this strange box than about him, strode angrily across the square to investigate.

"Stop playing these 'words of the devil'!" he ordered.

Before Martin could explain the words were from God, not the devil, the priest had grabbed the record from Martin's hand and smashed it. Jabbing his finger in Martin's face he warned,

"Don't play any more records with Martin Luther's lies!"

Martin shrugged in resignation. "The *padre* doesn't want to believe God's Word."

Drawn by the altercation, a crowd of half-drunk *fiesta*-goers gathered about Martin.

"Play the records for us," they insisted.

Not wishing to risk the destruction of his spare records, Martin shook his head.

"Not here. I will go to your home and play so the women and children can hear, too," he offered.

Single file, the men from Corralito led the way out of town, through tasseled cornfields, across a rushing river and on to the opposite bank, to a large hut. Two wildly barking dogs dashed out of the open doorway to snap at the heels of the stranger until silenced by a stick.

Smoke seeped under the eaves of the Mucha family's hut which housed fourteen people. Nearby a small corncrib stood with a plank tied in place with vines for a door. Beyond the corncrib was a low, domed family steambath plastered with mud. A few clay water jugs stood outside. Just below the eaves hung a hollow log, mudded at each end, containing a swarm of wild bees.

Quickly the women and children gathered to watch, wide-eyed, as Martin carefully lowered his load to the ground. He never allowed anyone else to carry his victrola because once the strap had broken and the victrola had fallen to the ground.

"The devil did that, because he knows that the little victrola tells us God's Word even when there is no one else to tell us," he explained seriously.

Several months previous, I had recorded Psalm 115 with Gospel Recordings in Mexico City. The words were powerful.

Our God is in heaven,
Whatever His heart wanted,
He has made.
Their false gods are made of silver and gold
by man's hands.
They have mouths but they don't speak.
They have eyes but they don't see.
They have ears but they don't hear.
They have noses but they can't smell anything.
They have hands but they don't move.
They have feet but they don't walk.
They have throats but they are not able to talk.
Those who make these false gods,
and those who trust in them,
are just like them.

His long legs stretched out before him as he sat on the ground beside the talking box, Martin added his word to what the record had said.

"It is true, what it says. Our patron saint has eyes but cannot see. He has ears but cannot hear. He has a mouth but cannot talk. He has feet but cannot walk. It is just as the record says."

In consternation, the Muchas looked at each other. It was unthinkable that Santo Tomas was not God! They had never dared think such a thing, let alone voice it! Here in their own language, was a record telling them there is a living God in heaven who does see and hear and speak.

Again and again, Martin cranked the victrola and replayed the record.

"Did you hear what it said?" Martin reiterated. "The saints aren't alive. In vain, we buy candles, incense and firerockets to worship them. In vain, we spend large sums in order to be *capitán* of a *fiesta*. God says our souls aren't saved that way."

Juan felt his heart racing. For years, he had dreamed of being a *fiesta capitán* as had his father and grandfather before him. His grandfather had told him that if a man hadn't served the saints here on earth, God would not allow him into heaven. Juan had learned to distill liquor from sugarcane juice in order to provide the many jugs of liquor required of him when the day came for him to be *capitán*. He had already chosen which saint he was going to serve; the one called "Our Lord God." With its vivid coloring and flowing robes, it looked alive and Juan felt this saint could assure salvation. Now the record said all that was useless. It struck a responsive chord in his heart.

Martin turned the record over and played the other side to the transfixed audience.

"The sun isn't alive. The sun isn't God. But there is a living God who made the sun and moon and put them up in the sky. He made us, too. And because we hurt very much in His heart, He sent His Son to save us."

Trying to grasp the full import of the words, Juan sensed that questions which had long burned in his own heart were finding answers. Ever since he was young, Juan had yearned to know God. Often he had lain on his back under the open sky, hoping to get a glimpse of God. All his efforts to know God had left his questions unanswered and his heart unsatisfied. The Tzeltal word for "thirsty" translates as "my heart is dry." If the message on the record was true, then perhaps...

All night Martin wound and rewound his victrola for the Mucha family. The children had long before succumbed to sleep while the elders remained around the victrola, listening with awe.

One record ended with a song. Martin reached into his bandana kerchief and drew out a well-thumbed hymnbook. From it he read the words of the song in Tzeltal. Juan and his cousin Domingo crowded closer following his finger as he pointed out word after word. They had thought the language of the *mestizos* was the only one which could be written down on paper. This was their own language! Martin pieced in from memory the words he couldn't actually read. Then he taught them the songs.

Though the Indians rarely sang except for some ribald drinking rhymes, they were quick to learn to carry a tune.

A rooster's crow announced the dawn. Martin and the Mucha family had been up all night. It was time for him to return home.

"Don't lose God's Word out of your hearts," he warned as he started off on his long day's trek into the mountains.

Both Juan and Domingo held offices in the Oxchuc church. They held keys to the church door since one of their duties entailed "the care of the saints." One day the cousins walked to Oxchuc together with a mission in mind.

Across from the dingy town hall loomed a massive seventeenth century church. As Juan and Domingo stepped inside, the smell of stale incense and decaying flowers assailed their nostrils. High over the central altar, stern Santo Tomas ruled over the less important saints who were lined up against both walls of the cavernous church. It was irreverently rumored that one of the lady saints was Santo Tomas' wife.

In spite of the record's words about "false gods", the men were nervous. Still, they had to know.

In trepidation, they began to examine the saints. In the past, they had not dared to lift their eyes to look closely at these figures for fear of displaying a lack of respect.

"Look, the paint is chipped off this one," they commented in low tones to one another.

"This one has a finger broken off and you can see what kind of wood it is made out of!"

"The dust is thick on this one's face. He can't be alive!"

Bolder and bolder they grew as they passed along the line of saints. Daringly, Juan lifted up the floor-length robe of a pious-looking image. The torso was held up by a tripod.

"It looks just like the three-legged stool our women use to pat out *tortillas*!" they chortled.

Finally, they were standing before mighty Santo Tomas himself. When the children of Oxchuc were small, their parents held them up to kiss the hem of Santo Tomas' robe but they had been instructed not to look him directly in the face for fear he would strike them dead.

Now testing the words of the record, they were emboldened to look directly at him. Nothing happened. Further encouraged, Juan climbed up on the altar to get a better look.

He gasped to Domingo, "Santo Tomas is split down the back! There's a rat's nest in the crack!"

Could that have happened to the true God? Surely not! What the record said was true! Their conclusion was immediate.

"Then we ought to believe all that the records tell us," they decided.

With true conviction, they let themselves out of the "house of false gods" as they called it ever after, released from the prison they had so long endured. Never again did they set foot in the Oxchuc church.

Juan was impatient to pursue this first glimpse of the true God. He would have departed immediately in search of the *gringas* to ask them many questions. But there were fourteen mouths to feed and with the coming of the dry season, he had to make a large clearing for a cornfield. Bent double, with the sun beating on their backs, he and Domingo spent day after day hacking down the underbrush with their *machetes*. But at midday, when they stopped work to drink a gourdful of the corn gruel brought to them by their wives, their conversation unfailingly turned to "God's Word" brought to them by faithful Martin Gourd.

When Holy Week was over, Juan, Domingo and three other men from Corralito wrapped large balls of freshly-ground corn gruel in a banana leaf and started off before the sun had risen to light their way.

It was a four-hour walk to Oxchuc, straight up the mountain. Several more hours elapsed before they reached Incense-Burner Spring where Martin Gourd lived. The mid-afternoon had caught them in a cold, unremitting drizzle. It made no difference. They insisted that Martin take them directly to *me'tik*'s house an hour and a quarter farther down the mountainside. In his net bag, Juan had also brought with him a pencil and a sheet of notebook paper so that he could write down "all that God has said." He had no idea of the length of the Bible nor did he realize that he was the one chosen of God to help *me'tik* translate it into his own language during the next five years.

With the five men from Corralito trailing behind him, Martin appeared at our door late that rainy afternoon.

"*Me'tik*, these are the ones from Corralito whose hearts like God's Word. They have come to hear more," he told us. Unmindful of their wet clothes and muddy feet, they looked at us expectantly as the ones who had God's Book and could tell them more about Him.

One of the men fished into his net bag and pulled out a well-thumbed hymnbook, the one Martin had left with them months before.

"Do you have more of these?" he asked.

I nodded. "Yes, we have a copy for each of you. Would you like to learn the hymns in Tzeltal?"

I started to teach them the first hymn in the little book. They already knew it. Next page. They knew that one, too. Every single hymn in that booklet they had memorized - at least the words, if not the tune!

Amazed, I opened the Gospel of Mark in Tzeltal and started to read it to them.

"I know how to read," volunteered Juan. "God willed it so that I would be able to read His Word."

Reverently, he took the printed portion in his hands and read a few verses aloud. The words came painstakingly slow because Juan was earnestly attempting to get every syllable perfect. We discovered he had also taught his older brother Mariano and his cousin Domingo to read so they would be able to read God's Word for themselves when they returned to Corralito. From the hundreds in Oxchuc who did not know one letter from another, the Lord sent us three who could read!

As elated as we over his five converts from Corralito, Martin was tasting the joy of having won others to "*like precious faith*" in Christ. He had been the first believer among the Yochib Tzeltals and had borne the brunt of the persecution. Not only had Juan Nich threatened his life many times but he had slashed him with a *machete* and left a long scar on his arm.

Martin appointed himself tour guide of our house. He proudly pointed out all our wonderful belongings: victrola, radio, accordion, Viewmaster pictures of our land. And he briefed them on our life and customs:

"*Me'tik* Lorensa knows how to give medicine. If you hurt anywhere, she will treat you and you will get well," he affirmed from personal experience.

"And *me'tik* Marianna is the one who puts God's Word into our words. She has had God's Book all her life and her father and grandfather had it, too. Those in the *Estados Unidos* are not like us. We have never heard about the real, living God because there is no one to tell us."

The afternoon lengthened into evening. Our guests continued to be absorbed in the things of God. And we continued to marvel. In contrast to the apathy of the Yochib people who yawned in our faces when we talked to them about the Lord, we were beginning to see a response to the Spirit of God. It was more refreshing than I can describe.

It was after nine that night before sleepiness began to get the better of our visitors. Reluctantly, they followed Martin up the trail to his hut for the night. Martin told us later that they stayed up several more hours, talking over everything they had heard that memorable day while examining the Gospels, the Bible Story books and the hymnals we had given them.

Ten days later, Florence and I were startled to see a long line of people streaming down the mountainside to our house; nine men and boys, five women and three babies! With Juan in the lead, they had come to hear for themselves "the Word of the Lord."

They arrived in a drenching downpour. Unlike Indian huts, our house didn't have a roaring fire in the middle of the floor for them to dry out. Their spirits were not dampened by the rain or by the long trip over the trail. From four o'clock that afternoon until ten o'clock that night they listened, enthralled, to all that we told them from the Word of God. Some sat on benches, others sat crosslegged on the floor drinking in every word and gazing intently at the flannelgraph figures as we illustrated the stories. Never had we seen anyone so famished to hear the Word of God!

The story of Creation, the Fall, the Flood but especially the three believers from the Book of Daniel impressed them as they heard of God's mighty deliverance from the fiery furnace.

"We ought not to bow before the idols, either, no matter what happens to us," they concluded.

"Now that we know where the living God is, we ought to believe in Him."

The women took us aside to squat beside us, cradling their babies in their arms. They wanted to repeat the words of the hymns to us "to see if we say it correctly." None of them could read but they knew every word in the hymnbook letter-perfect. The work of the Spirit was truly in evidence in their reception of spiritual truth. Compared to others among the Yochib people, the difference was almost disheartening for little light had penetrated Yochib hearts in spite of the years we had spent among them.

Our visitors finally settled for the night. The men and boys slept on the floor of the dispensary while the women and babies bedded down on the floor of our room. Somehow, a house that was built to accomodate two people stretched enough for nineteen!

When Florence opened to our nightly page of Daily Light, she was so tired the book fell into her bowl of soup. The pages were irremediably stuck together at that place forever after as a reminder of our exhilarating, exhausting day - the day Corralito came to us.

At dawn next morning, the Indians were astir wanting to hear the victrola records. They memorized passages from Scripture, learned songs and stored as much of the Word in their hearts as they could. Christ's death and resurrection were new to them. Their hearts were moved as they realized all He had done for their sakes!

The women, especially, did not want to leave. Holding our hands in their own, they begged us to pray for them and their husbands that they might "really believe on the Lord."

I wrote home to my parents,

This is the Lord's doing that they understand the Word so well and all that their new faith implies: no drinking, no bowing before idols, no giving of liquor for the bridal-price or offering it at the graves on the Day of the Dead...they are in earnest about following the Lord!

It was a responsiveness we had not seen in Yochib in the five years we had been there.

Early in the spring, Juan Nich and the schoolteacher began an all-out campaign to get us to leave Yochib. The teacher claimed he needed Villa's house for an addition to the school.

When Martin Gourd offered us some of his land if we wished to build on it, Juan Nich countered by threatening to bring a curse on him. The fear of the supernatural was everpresent even with these new believers and we realized that settling on land which belonged to a Christian would expose him to even more persecution than he had already suffered.

We had spent five years in Yochib. Though seeds had been sown, the results were pitifully few. There were over 45,000 other Tzeltals who had never heard the Gospel at all.

Interested inquirers from Tenejapa, as well as the Corralito group, indicated there might be more of a response elsewhere. Our lease would be terminated in October. The roof and fence needed repairs. Were all these circumstances indicators that we should consider a ministry elsewhere among the Tzeltals?

Then in June, we received a letter from Juan Mucha, dictated to a rancher who knew Spanish.

There are now many of us...perhaps seventy. All the men and women want you to come right away.

All the time, I play the victrola. Every Sunday, we gather ourselves together. Many now know the Word of God. Come and teach us more of God's Word. I will make you a house here so that you can teach us.

The invitation touched us deeply. After the many years we had been made to feel unwelcome, it was heartwarming to be wanted!

Florence planned to return to Canada for her second summer at SIL. I was enrolled at the University of Mexico for several Mayan courses which would better educate me in the history and culture of these Indians. Yet, we hated to leave these new believers without some strong foundation to continue on with the Lord.

We invited the new believers to meet us in Las Casas for a few days of Bible study where they could be away from the demands of home and farm so all could concentrate on the Word. Without any way of knowing how many would respond, we were overjoyed to find twenty-four eager students waiting for us at their first Bible Conference. There were five from Yochib, twelve from Corralito and seven others. The evangelical church in Las Casas allowed us to use their building.

"No saints!" the Indian believers whispered to one another, peering around the spacious, well-lit chapel. In place of the customary dust-covered images of the town church, a large open Bible was displayed on the pulpit. Florence played the wheezing antiquated organ as the Indians crowded around to sing their much-loved hymns.

On Saturday morning, we began with Bible stories from the Book of Mark. The Feeding of the Five Thousand strengthened their hearts for the months to come when corn might be scarce. The

accounts of Jesus healing the sick enabled Juan
to pray for healing for Mariano, his brother. The
words of the Lord through the storm, "*Fear not, I
am with you*" were to provide encouragement for
the days ahead when they would face opposition
as the first believers in the area.

That night twenty of our Bible students slept
side by side the whole length of the porch of the
home where we were staying with fellow missionaries. Some of them had gone over the new
songs again and again by the light of flashlights.
We heard some making plans with Martin to take
the Gospel to other parts of the tribe.

For their first Sunday service in a church, our
Indian friends filled three or four rows of benches.
Though the service was in Spanish and none of
them understood a word of it, they sat very still
for the entire two hours. What they did understand was that they were among those of "*like precious faith*" and had been made welcome.
Ordinarily, *mestizos* refused to mingle with Indians, calling them "dogs." But here, among the
evangelicals, the *mestizos* called the Tzeltals
"brethren."

Martin was always alert. He had forewarned his
friends of the offering and each was ready. They
unknotted their red sashes and took out a few
coins to contribute as their "gift to God." One of
the elders, humble, devout don Abelino, welcomed
the Tzeltals to the service in their own language.
The Indian Christians also sang some of the Tzeltal hymns for the congregation. Immediately after
the service, they were invited to have coffee and
sweet bread with their Spanish-speaking
brothers. It was the first time they had realized
that all over Mexico were "brothers" who were one
with them in Christ Jesus.

This is the generation
of them that seek Him. . .
Psalm 24:6

The promise of God -

it was all that carried me
through the turmoil
of indecision and bewilderment
in the months which followed.

Chapter Nine

Corralito

I was halfway through my courses at the University of Mexico that summer when my father wired me that Mother was critically ill. I offered to drop my studies immediately but Dad felt I should finish, then come home.

I arrived in Philadelphia at the end of my summer studies. The bustling, sophisticated city provided a sharp contrast to the slower pace of Mexican living. I felt a foreigner in my own land.

My father needed my support as much as he needed my help about the house. In spite of the strain which Mother's illness placed on us all, it was a time of drawing together as a family united in love and prayer.

Mother's illness was terminal and we had no way of knowing how long she would linger. It produced a dilemma of huge dimension to me. There was the biblical injunction to consider:

Honor thy father and mother.

I was the only single one in the family. Did I not owe these beloved elderly people a debt of obedience to be with them through the trying months which lay ahead?

But there was the lifelong commitment I had made to serve the Lord as a Bible translator. The Tzeltal New Testament was not yet finished.

Florence and I had proved to be thoroughly compatible partners. She needed my knowledge of Tzeltal in order to continue in the same area.

I felt like Jacob wrestling all night with the Angel. Wholeheartedly, I wanted to do what was right. But I didn't know which choice to make. There was the longing to help my parents and there was the call of my beloved Tzeltals.

In the end, my father made my decision for me.

There are thousands among your people who have never heard. We want you here with us. But more than that, we want to see many in heaven who might not be there if you stayed home.

He bought me a ticket to Mexico City. It was a tremendous wrench for us all. Like David, he "*would not offer to the Lord that which cost him nothing.*" The Lord was gracious in His reward to my parents for their sacrificial giving. Mother lived eleven more years and was able to visit me among the Tzeltals before she went on to be with Him.

I had been torn with indecision. I now passed into a calm, clear period of inner tranquility. In the words of that lovely hymn by George Caldbeck,

> *Peace, perfect peace,*
> *With loved ones far away?*
> *In Jesus' keeping I am safe - and they.*
> *Peace, perfect peace,*
> *The future all unknown?*
> *Jesus we know, And He is on the Throne!*

Don Abelino, the Mexican elder of the evangelical church in Las Casas where we had held our first Bible Conference in June, was eager to accompany Florence and me out to Corralito where we had been invited to live. Word had spread among the new believers that we had returned and a group of ten to twelve of them, along with Martin Gourd, had come in to Las Casas to conduct us out to their home. With a caravan of six mules, two riding horses, two mule drivers and seven Indian carriers, we headed out over a trail new to us. The earnest eagerness of the new believers made my family sacrifice abundantly worthwhile. As Florence and I rode along, both of us were given the confidence of heart that we were to care for Christ's "*other sheep*" while He marshalled His angels to be "*ministering spirits*" to my parents.

It was a two-day trail ride from Las Casas to Corralito. The closer we drew to our destination, the more believers came to meet us along the trail. Though some had never seen us, they greeted us as if they had known us all their lives. When we finally arrived at the little clearing, they led us to the little thatched hut which we were to occupy until they could build us a home of our own.

Anxiously, their eyes followed us as we investigated our new domain. Boards lashed in place with vines, two planks laid over forked sticks for beds, a large rustic chair which they had located and the dirt floor spread with fresh pine needles, all revealed their love and eagerness to please.

The Lord will build thee an house

was the promise the Lord had given me the day we headed for Corralito.

Juan led the group, at least seventy of them, in a welcoming circle of singing. From wrinkled old men down to little tots, they all sang the hymns from memory.

What a welcome! It was thrilling that we could all join in singing praises to the same God! Our lives and backgrounds were different but we shared the bond that unites.

The Corralito Tzeltals smothered us with loving kindness. They brought us water from the stream and gave us gifts of eggs and oranges. They brought a tiny table on which they set carefully-wrapped *tortillas* and two bowls with soft-boiled eggs and a cup of coffee for each of us. It was a true banquet prepared with loving hearts and hands.

The next day with men, women and children trailing behind us single file, we went to the spot on the Mucha clan's land they had chosen for our future home. Set in a clearing on a steep hillside, a spacious view spread before us on three sides. A rushing stream nearby provided all the water we would need. Beams and poles had already been cut for our home and work was begun as soon as we gave approval for the site.

We had not finished preparing breakfast over our one-burner "foxhole" stove when the people began to arrive for Sunday morning service. Florence got out the accordion and we all, without a single exception, sang through the entire hymnbook.

Under the open sky, they sat down while we told the flannelgraph story of Jesus. Eyes glistened with tears as I reached the part about His death on the Cross for their sins. Even the hardened older people responded. Don Abelino counted at least two hundred who listened for an hour to the whole story.

No boredom here, no passing it off as a small thing of little consequence - Jesus' sacrifice touched their hearts to the inmost core. There was a clamor of voices when I asked if they wanted us to live among them.

"Stay here and teach us the Word of God," said the older leader, Tomas Ch'ijk.

Forgetful of their food, most lingered all day with us. As the sky darkened, those who remained crowded into our little hut. We taught them some of the new songs I had translated. Juan Mucha moved us deeply as he told of the tremendous longing he had always had for God even before he heard of Him. In unison, we all prayed the prayer I had included in the hymnal. It was sweet to hear these new believers thank the Lord for sending someone to tell them about Him,

"Because otherwise we would never have heard and we would have been lost."

Sunday services in Corralito lasted at least five hours. Some Indians lived so far away that they came the day before in order to be on hand for the Sunday service. Deprived as they had been for generations, it was a thrill to them to learn that God was recording their names in the Book of Life!

Almost every night our little hut was filled to overflowing with believers who wanted to sing and talk about the Lord. Early in December as we gathered, we had something special on our hearts. Word had come from Martin that the old chiefs of the tribe planned to summon him to Oxchuc. In punishment for having "ruined the whole tribe" (many no longer worshipped Santo Tomas), the tribal leaders planned to kill Martin before them all. Included in this news was the information that the old chiefs of the tribe had burned huge candles before Santo Tomas, beseeching him to get rid of the *gringas* - us.

On a *fiesta* day when most of the traditional officials of the tribe were getting drunk, Martin appeared from Yochib with a borrowed rifle over his
shoulder. He was filled with fear and he needed
help to "*trust and not be afraid.*"

The summons to appear before the tribal chiefs
in Oxchuc never came. Perhaps it had been an
idle threat or perhaps the Lord intervened and
weakened their resolve to do away with him.

As threats of persecution grew so did the reports
of believers turning to the Lord. In a nearby
rancheria, two believers who could read borrowed
our victrola and took it from hut to hut to tell of
the Gospel. From that small witness came a number of new converts to worship with the believers
of Corralito.

When we mimeographed three hundred new
copies of the hymnal with its bright red cover, they
were sold within four days. A hymnal became the
Indians' most prized possession. They kept it
carefully wrapped in a kerchief and would pull it
from their net bags or from inside their shirt
fronts, carefully holding it with one corner of their
kerchief so it would not become finger-marked.
Most of them could not read yet but they had
memorized all the words, page by page, line by
line.

In letters to my parents, I wrote,

*It is wonderful to have no drunkenness, no steal-
ing, no fear in hearts - the Lord has truly "crowned
this year with His goodness!" Your prayers have
brought it all to pass!*

*Christmas Day was the most blessed we have
ever had! Many came on Christmas Eve and
stayed overnight with us. The house was full to the
brim with the overflow spilling onto the porch:*

thirty-eight persons in all! We have never been alone in our hut a single night! The believers are so afraid that we might be lonely that they come to keep us company bringing babies, blankets, gourds and, of course, hymnals! There are always people with hymnals in hand, waiting to sing, some on the porch bending over the reading charts, others getting medicine from Florence, youngsters playing with our rubber ball in the yard...

Christmas morn people began arriving in hordes, all of them greeting us both Indian fashion, and commenting on the fact that we were wearing Indian clothes like theirs! Martin Gourd and Martin K'ux came all the way from Yochib for the first Christmas in Corralito. There must have been more than three hundred gathered in our yard as we began to sing the songs plus about fifteen Mexicans, some of them believers, who later arrived to spend Christmas Day with us, too. I set up the manger scene you gave me and to an attentive audience, explained about the first coming of the Lord and then about His second coming. Juan Mucha, to whom the Lord's coming is a very real, precious fact, seconded my words, giving a wonderful explanation of the things God's Word says concerning both the first and second coming which I had explained to him just the day before! He is a chosen one of the Lord with spiritual understanding that I can only say "flesh and blood hath not revealed it unto him, but the Lord...by His spirit."

The believers gave an offering as their "gift to God" to be sent to Gospel Recordings so others can hear of Him as they have. We have had to mimeograph 250 more hymnals to supplement the 250 we have already sold because the demand is so great. This is the revival you've been asking the Lord to send among the Tzeltals.

This week we revised I John with some of the believers coming to help in the revision three nights of the week. I wish you could see us gathered around the table with our heads bent over His Word! Juan Mucha is the Lord's chosen one for the translation - spiritually keen! And he puts in his heart every word of God's Word, then gives it out to others.

In just a short time, Juan Mucha had learned to type on my machine in his own language and proved to be quite accurate, even to the glottal stops. He sent a letter to my parents,

Very esteemed Father and Mother:

I greet your hearts very much in the Name of our Lord God. Thank you for your card you sent me. I was very much comforted by it. Therefore, I send you a little note. Also, I want you to hear that we have believed the Word of God so that you may be comforted, too. Also, I want to greet your hearts. Thank you for the way in which the Word of God has come to us. That is what I want to say to you. Also, I want to tell you how many of us have believed the Word of God. There are many of us. There are three hundred. I want to tell you so that you may be glad because of it. We thank God that we are now in His hand. I have truly believed well the Word of God. So we thank God.

Juan Mucha

Surely each generation has its man especially chosen of God. For the Tzeltals at Corralito, that man was Juan Mucha. He was only twenty-two when he first heard the Gospel from Martin's recordings. At that young age, he was the sole support of his wife, two infant sons, his widowed mother and all her younger children, fourteen people in all. In addition, because his older

brother Mariano was sickly, he helped to contribute to that household. He had received very
little education but his keen mind grasped
spiritual truths immediately in a way few Christians do. Unusually sensitive to the needs of
others, Juan wanted others to know the Lord as
soon as he found Him. When he entered the
house, the whole room lit up. His energetic, fun-
loving nature made him a joy to work with. From
the very first, there was a genuine bond of trust
and love between us. Night after night after a hard
day's work in his cornfields, Juan would come to
our house to help translate the Gospel of John.
Never have I seen anyone so excited about each
nugget of wisdom as Juan! Sometimes, we would
hear a sudden shout, startling us as we bent over
our translation. Juan was keeping himself from
falling asleep by giving a loud yell. It worked for
the rest of us, as well!

Early in his experience, he realized that love was
the crux of all Christian living. One time, he
pulled me aside to ask a serious question:

"*Me'tik*, you have had God's Word all your life?
And your father and grandfather before you?"

"Yes."

"God's Word says we must love everybody. Do
you love everyone? There is one man I don't love.."

His earnestness convicted me. Juan set high
standards for himself and he held others to equally high standards. Though he was young and the
Tzeltals looked to older men for leadership, he was
a natural leader commanding great respect in all
his contacts. He dealt as a pastor with his people.
When they presented themselves to him for baptism, he tested them rigorously on the condition
of their hearts.

"Do you still get angry?"

"Are you at one heart with your wife?"

Not only was Juan a pioneer in the Christian faith, he also pioneered in practical problems of daily living. He was the first among the Tzeltals to do away with the old "slash-and-burn" method of farming and implement terraced cornfields instead. He learned to make wheelbarrows and even rigged up a telephone out of old cans to the house of his cousin which actually worked!

In all the time the Lord was testing me for obedience and perseverance, He was preparing this humble servant of the Lord for a mighty share in His kingdom, the translation of the New Testament into Tzeltal. What if I had stayed home that summer when Mother was so ill? Here was the abundant harvest the Lord had planned among the Tzeltals!

The men had quickly erected a new one-room hut for us, with a high, sweet-smelling grass roof, mud walls and fresh pine needles on the ground. Florence's little dispensary was at one end under a window. A row of shoulder-high boxes divided that area off from our living quarters. Every night, we had overnight guests sleeping on mats at the foot of our cots. Sometimes a sick person who wanted us "to talk to God" for him, would see the Lord honor his faith by healing him.

Several times each week, as many as thirty different people would crowd into our house to listen in as Juan and I worked on the translation of John. They were very quiet, listening intently. When we tried out a new phrase on them, there would be much discussion among them as to what it really meant and a consensus had to be agreed on before we passed on to the next passage. My

Tzeltal vocabulary grew and the Tzeltals grew in their knowledge of the Word for they not only heard it, they helped translate it and they hid it in their hearts. It was a vital key to transformed lives and customs.

Unlike English, the Tzeltal language makes no distinction between the words "to believe" and "to obey." It was quite possibly this very lack of distinction which made their conversion to the Lord so complete. To them, to believe on the Lord meant to obey the Lord!

Our translation of "the Lord" was *Cajwaltic*, meaning "our owner." They took seriously the fact that now they belonged wholly to the Lord.

Our days were more than full. In preparation for the evening sessions for translation, I spent many hours of the day studying the exegesis of the passage we planned to cover that night. With the primers we had prepared in Yochib, we taught the people to read, one by one and in small groups. It was necessary that they have simple reading material before they could comprehend the New Testament.

The enthusiasm of these eager disciples more than made up for the years of discouragement in Yochib.

This people have I formed for Myself;
they shall show forth My praise.
                                    Isaiah 43:21

January, 1950
introduced
a year
of
new beginnings.

Chapter Ten

New Beginnings

So quickly did the Corralito Tzeltals absorb the meaning of the New Testament that they needed little transition from the old ways to the new. They, who had been so steeped in superstition and witchcraft, dropped both with the great relief of leaving prison and breathing in the fresh air of freedom. The heavy drinking expected of all Tzeltal men at every occasion, ceased. The Mucha family led the way. When invited to participate in the wedding celebration of a relative, they declined saying they wanted no part in the drunkenness. As a result, some of that branch of the family came to hear of the Lord for the first time. The Gospel was spreading through the mountains like wildfire!

Since it is not the policy of Wycliffe Bible Translators to found churches, it was necessary for the new Christians to be affiliated very quickly with a larger body of believers. Florence and I did not want them to feel they were complete aliens in the world but to know there were many other believers in Mexico. Since the Presbyterians were the evangelical representatives in the State of Chiapas, it was to this church that the leaders turned. In mid-January, the evangelical church in Las Casas sent out Daniel Aguilar, their pastor, and don Abelino, to visit the expanding congregation. The blessings were reciprocal for Daniel brought them greetings of encouragement from the "elder brethren" in Las Casas and the enthusiasm of the new Indian Christians was a tremendous thrill to the two men.

Francisco Nimail, a schoolteacher, interpreted well for don Daniel's sermon, "*My son, give me thy heart.*"

Don Daniel then explained to the two hundred and fifty gathered on the hillside the seriousness of Christian baptism as a testimony of their faith.

For the formation of a church, each married member would have to be legally married according to Mexican law. This was an unheard of thing for illiterate mountain Indians! It would pose problems for some of the men had two wives. There were at least eighty couples who would have to be legally married if they were to participate in the Corralito congregation.

The believers unanimously elected their first president, Juan Mucha. When we listed the names of those who were candidates for baptism, we found there were over four hundred counting the children! This large number had grown from only seventy when we had first come to Corralito three months before. We knew we would be very busy preparing the new believers for the return of Daniel Aguilar and don Abelino in just six months. At that time, those applying for membership would be examined for an understanding of Christian faith and its application in daily living.

In the year before Florence and I came to Corralito, Tomás Ch'ijk had lost five of his children. His face deeply seamed with grief, he had come out of great darkness for he was a *shaman* and had dealt with Satan's allies. Tomás Ch'ijk was an impressive man. Of stocky build and pleasant demeanor, he had an air of authority about him. He had developed his distinctive personality through the years of being revered by the Indians who came to him for assistance. *Shamans* could do good as well as evil and much of the fear generated about them was spread by super- stitious rumor rather than by any true deeds. Tomás was the one who made the Mayan cross for each family to worship in their own homes.

On one of Martin Gourd's previous trips out from Yochib with the victrola, he had come to Tomás Ch'ijk's house. Hesitating, for he still feared the power of witchcraft, Martin asked if he could play the records for the old man and his wife. Both agreed readily. Their response to the mes- sage surprised even Martin for they believed as soon as they heard. Their hearts had been sof- tened through the deaths of their children and they thirsted for the comfort only Christ's love can give.

Tomás was among the first to welcome us at Corralito and he was faithful in attendance at every meeting. In the beginning, some were a bit suspicious of his presence for fear he was a spy seeing who claimed to be Christians. But Tomás was as sincere as anyone and truly loved the Lord.

One day he took us aside, looking furtively over both shoulders to see that we were not overheard. He lowered his voice to confide an important mat- ter - his daughter, Magdala, had been asked for in marriage. The widow, Bana, had made five trips to his hut with gifts of food, five successive Fridays at dawn, to ask for a wife for her son.

"Is it all right in God's sight to give my daughter to the widow Bana's son?" he asked anxiously.

"It is all right," we assured him, "if you asked God first and if you asked Magdala if she is will- ing."

His expression betrayed the novelty of that idea to him!

With his hand raised to his mouth uncertainly, he posed the next question,

"But would it be all right in God's sight to accept liquor for the bride price?"

Tribal custom dictated the price of a wife to be four large jugs of liquor from the husband's family to all the girl's clan relatives.

This was precedent-setting for what was decided for this first Christian wedding would determine the conduct of weddings for the years to come. The young Christian leaders gathered to discuss the matter with great gravity. The consensus of opinion was given to Tomás Ch'ijk.

"Now that you belong to God, you cannot accept liquor for your daughter. Your son-in-law, who also belongs to God, cannot give you liquor in exchange for his wife. Tell him to buy fresh meat with the money he would have spent for liquor."

Tomás readily agreed to follow what the younger men said "God's heart wanted."

The day of the wedding under a merciless March sun, we toiled up the steep mountain trail to old Tomás' hut. Thirty families of the old man's clan had gathered for the occasion. The dark looks and surly voices of the unbelievers betrayed their anger at the lack of liquor. But then their eyes wandered to the whole cow which had been slaughtered for the feast, the huge quantities of ground corn and baskets stacked high with hundreds of *tortillas* for the wedding feast.

Juan Mucha had never seen a Christian wedding ceremony but he wanted this one to honor the Lord and to be based on His Word. With his well-used Gospel of Mark open to chapter ten, he adjured both the newlyweds and the family on both sides to obey the Word of God. The new son-in-law would serve his wife's parents for a year before he would be allowed to take his wife home. He would not be permitted to leave her if she was lazy. She would not be allowed to go back to her parents if she felt lonely. God's Word pronounced them one.

Old Tomás punctuated Juan's words with, "Hear, hear what God says." His eyes circled the wedding guests to see what impression God's Word was making.

The young couple then knelt on the ground while Juan earnestly asked the Lord's blessing on them. The non-believers of the old man's clan looked ill at ease but not one of them dared protest the substitution of a Christian ceremony for the familiar pagan rites.

The sun had cooled and the distant peaks were beginning to turn mauve when the wedding guests bade old Tomás goodbye and left for their scattered huts. In their hemp bags were generous portions of fresh meat and ground corn for their families at home. A far cry from the customary drunken dissipation of the past!

Glancing over our shoulders as we started down the trail, we saw the sheepish young bridegroom following us and a discreet distance behind him, his shy young bride.

So thirsty for God's Word were the Corralito believers that a four- or five-hour service was routine every Sunday. Dressed in their best hand-woven garments with bright bands of red and orange embroidery around the neck and sleeves, they arranged themselves about the hilly ground. Occasionally, when a fussing child distracted others, the speaker would point to the mother and order, "Feed your baby!"

If someone found himself sleepy, he would stand up and stretch so he would not nod off. The Word of God was too important for them to miss by napping.

They never tired of the songs and the reading of God's Word provoked much animated discussion. The Word never became stale to them for they took it home with them and the message became the yardstick for their behavior through the week. They were constantly winning new people and, with the influx of new converts, their Christian lives did not become stagnant.

One Sunday, Alonzo Morales and his grown son, Marcos, lingered after the rest had started homeward. Alonzo was a greatly-feared *shaman* with many enemies stemming from land feuds in the past. His expression was mask-like and he rarely smiled. Yet, he and his two wives had been faithful in attending services ever since we had come to Corralito though they lived a half-hour away. Although some were still afraid of his power to practice witchcraft, he seemed to have "turned his heart to God."

"*Me'tik*, teach me the new hymn," he requested, almost timidly. We started to teach him.

> *Our Lord is coming soon,*
> *Let us be waiting for Him.*

Alonzo found it hard to learn the simple words. He shook his head.

"It doesn't remain in my heart. I guess my heart is thick. Tell me again," he repeated.

We were touched by his determination to learn
"God's song." He persevered until he had learned
the chorus and finally, late in the afternoon, he
took his leave.

Alonzo and Marcos had been gone only a half
hour when a young woman came running up the
trail to our house, chanting the death wail. A chill
of apprehension came over us as we recognized
Rosa Ch'ishna who lived at Alonzo's house. Distraught, she caught hold of us and sobbed:

"He is dead! Alonzo is dead! They killed him!"
She broke into a mournful wail.

From Rosa's disconnected account, we pieced
together what had occurred. Halfway to his hut,
in a narrow pass where the trail is hemmed in on
both sides by underbrush, Alonzo had been ambushed by an enemy of the past as he and Marcos talked about the "good new words" they had
heard that day. The bullets, fired at close range,
had barely missed Marcos who was a few paces
behind him. Alonzo had lunged a few steps farther after he had been hit then crumpled to the
ground, dead. We were the last ones to have seen
him alive. And his last words had been of the
Lord's soon coming.

Alonzo, feared by all and befriended by few
during his lifetime, was the first of the new
believers to die. His Christian brethren gathered
from all over to give him the first Christian funeral
in Corralito.

On a treeless hilltop where Alonzo's relatives
and neighbors watched over the corpse, we congregated to comfort the grieving family. His jaw
tied shut with a red bandana kerchief, Alonzo lay
with hands folded on his chest, two lighted
candles at his head. Outside, the women sat

crosslegged on the ground, talking in hushed tones while the men dug the grave nearby. They had sat up all night with the dead man's family.

The atmosphere was tense as the non-Christians disputed with the Christians as to how the burial should be conducted.

The unbelievers insisted, "We will send for someone to play the harp" (customary at Indian wakes and accompanied by drinking).

"No, we will play the records and sing the hymns our brother Alonzo liked," stated the believers just as firmly.

"We must buy liquor for the gravediggers with the money he left," the unbelievers decided.

"No, his wives and children need it now that they have been bereaved," the believers ruled, over protest.

Someone took his Mayan cross from its place on the low household altar facing the doorway.

"Throw it in the fire," old Tomás Ch'ijk ordered. He had been the most noted crossmaker in the region but he no longer believed it had magical powers. As the cross crackled and sputtered in the fire, Tomás added,

"That doesn't mean the cross is alive. It just means it is seasoned wood!"

The believers took charge at the graveside, ignoring the muttered comments of the others. Ranging themselves on either side of the open grave, they watched silently as Alonzo's bullet-riddled body, wrapped in a straw mat, was lowered respectfully into it. When one of the widows asked if she should bring Alonzo's hat, blanket, drinking gourd and other personal possessions to put in the grave, the believers said,

"No, he won't need them in heaven where he has gone."

Juan announced, "We will sing,

> *'There's no crying where Jesus is,*
> *There's no sadness....*
> *There's no death...*
> *There where Jesus is...'"*

Alonzo's widows suppressed their sobs while we all sang from memory. The hymns seemed made for this very moment. The Word of God had not come too late for Alonzo.

The unbelievers, thwarted from holding the customary pagan funeral, drifted away. The believers started homeward for the first time not afraid the dead man's spirit would come back to harm them. Hearts that had known only abysmal fear of death were comforted for they knew it is written in God's Word,

> *Whosoever believeth on Him,*
> *though he were dead, yet shall he live.*

Newly translated into Tzeltal, the words had fresh meaning to us all.

Land and working the cornfields were essential to the Tzeltals. Yet, they were eager to have more of the Word of God in their own language. Since Juan Mucha had such a large family to provide for, some of the men agreed among themselves to work his fields for him three days a week, to enable him to spend more hours with me on translation. It was an inspiration of the Holy Spirit for the first draft of the Gospel of John was completed that spring and we started on the Book of Acts by early June.

The early Christian church was being re-enacted in the lives of all around us while we translated Acts and terminology needed was taken right out of the lives of new believers and went immediately into the Tzeltal New Testament. It was forged directly from experience, not written in the isolation of a quiet study far removed from actual living.

From ancient Mayan times, the traditional requirements of planting had been followed faithfully. In January and February, the fields were cut and the dry brush burned. Whole hillsides were left scorched and over the blackened earth hung a pall of smoke which dimmed the rays of the sun.

The Tzeltals from miles around were expected to offer special prayers to St. Thomas in the Oxchuc church in a service called a *misa*. As part of the synthesis of Catholic and pagan belief, St. Thomas had been equated with the Mayan corn god. Following the March and April plantings, prayers and money had to be offered to St. Thomas or he would withhold the rain.

This year, the Corralito believers were determined to do it differently. Instead of traveling the four hours to Oxchuc and sacrificing to a god of wood, the Christians decided to commit their fields to the Lord's keeping.

The religious leaders in Oxchuc were furious. They predicted disaster on all the corn crops if the believers did not join their relatives in proffering St. Thomas his customary tribute. The money was needed to purchase firerockets, candles and liquor. The custom had been to shoot off the firerockets at the mouth of sacred caves while worshippers chanted prayers to restrain the heavy winds. The candles were to have been lighted before St. Thomas as the Indians beseeched him to grant a good crop. The liquor was necessary to fortify the *shamans* for dealing with the supernatural for they could not approach the deities without being intoxicated.

"Do you expect Santo Tomas to feed you when you don't pay him for it?" they taunted the new Christians when they refused to contribute to the pagan rites.

"The living God whom we have believed, will care for our cornfields," the believers retorted.

Marcos Ensin, tribal chief of the Oxchuc region, came in for his share of the blame. He had allowed Martin to play the records in his house and his own son had believed "the lies of the foreigners." Now, with the angry threats of the leaders and *shamans* in his ears, he decided to see for himself if the living God is in heaven. If so, he wanted to believe, too.

Juan Mucha, pioneer in so many of the Christian enterprises, determined that his planting that spring would be a Christian service. Early in March, a group of from ten to twenty men, each with a long, metal-tipped planting stick in one hand and selected seedcorn in a net bag on his hip, moved rhythmically across each field in even rows. With every step, they jabbed the ash-covered earth with their dibble-sticks, dropped four kernels of seedcorn into each hole and then moved on. After each field had been planted, they gathered together to sing "God's songs" and to commit their cornfields to the Lord's prospering rather than praying to the earth as they had previously done.

The women had worked for several days to make huge clay pots full of sour corn-gruel, heaped-up baskets of *tortillas* and enough hard-boiled eggs and blistering hot chili sauce to feed all the hungry workers. Before they sat down to eat, however, Domingo Mucha stood up with the Gospel of Mark in his hand, and read the Parable of the Sower.

"Brothers, we know how sad we are when the seed we plant does not grow. God is sad, too, when we don't heed His Word as we should."

Several of those intent on his words drew in their breath with a sharp click to show they were convicted by what Domingo said. He continued,

"You know that our cornfields yield different kinds of corn. Some ears have only a few grains and are not good for anything. Others are under-developed and only good for feeding to our animals. Others are good enough to store for food for our families in the year ahead. And others - the large, fully-formed ears - we tie together and hang over the rafters of our huts for next year's seedcorn. In the same way, there are different kinds of Christians. May we not disappoint the One Who planted His Word in our hearts. May we be His seedcorn."

His sermon ended, Domingo led in prayer, "Lord, You Who multiplied the five *tortillas* and two fishes to feed five thousand people long ago, can multiply the seed we have just planted to feed us."

Conscious that they would be blamed for lack of rain, he added fervently, "Lord, send the rains."

Before everyone had finished feasting, there was a sharp thunderclap and ominous-looking clouds began to scud across the sky. We had barely reached our house when the first drenching rains spattered over the parched earth! It was one of the best planting seasons the Tzeltals had had for many years!

After the many months of constant labor on their cornfields, mid-summer allowed the Tzeltals a welcome respite. It was then that they decided to build a chapel for the Lord for it would not be appropriate for over three hundred believers now gathering each Sunday to remain out of doors when the cold rains came. For these who had worshipped at every cave and waterhole, a chapel only for the Lord was an immense thrill. Francisco, a leader in the congregation, asked the men to line up if they were willing to work on the chapel. All the able-bodied men and boys formed into a line. Some had planned to go off to the coffee ranches on the coast for extra money but they readily agreed to stay and help with the building of the chapel.

A sightly hilltop was selected and donated by the families of the Kituk lineage - a costly sacrifice for every inch was valued for corn planting. The first week in August, a hundred men gathered on the hilltop to start work, *machetes* in hand. But when they started to dig holes for the row of posts that would support the framework, they discovered the hilltop was almost solid rock. Some wanted to abandon the location and look for another.

"No, let's talk to God about it," the leaders suggested. They knelt and asked the Lord to help them build their chapel on that hilltop. With a borrowed crowbar or two, they went to work with a will. When the going became difficult, they would kneel down again around the holes they were trying to dig and pray.

Most of them had never seen an evangelical chapel. The Oxchuc church was modeled after a cathedral of the seventeenth century. The Corralito believers designed this chapel ninety feet long and twenty-six feet wide with a door at either end. Florence and I let them decide the size and shape but we did suggest windows in each side and a platform across the far end with a pulpit for the preacher.

Since no building materials were available near the chapel, it was necessary to drag poles long distances over the trail. Countless trips, weighted down under huge bundles of grass for the roof, were the assignments of others. The pliable vines to tie the framework together had to be gathered from miles away. While the men worked on the framework and maneuvered the rafters into place, the women gathered nearby to pray that the Lord would keep them from falling and hurting themselves.

Finally in November, the new *templo* was ready to be dedicated - "placed before God." The minister of the Las Casas church, Daniel Aguilar, and one of the dedicated elders made the trip by horseback to be present. The chapel had been artistically decorated with arches of palm fronds from the forest.

With our shoes muddy from the still-wet floor, we stood on the platform and looked into a sea of Indian faces. Tears welled into our eyes as we recalled all these "trophies of grace" - each with a beautiful story of change in their lives.

Former *shaman* Tomás, no longer chanting but singing unto the Lord.

Former persecutor Yol, now listening to the Word of God.

Former pulsetaker Jacinto, with his entire family in church.

Former drunkard Sebastian, now sober and smiling.

Former bigamist Lek' who had sent back his second wife in obedience to God's Word.

And in the very front, for the first time, was Nicolás Nich with his large family, wanting everyone to know that "he had turned his heart to God."

Juan stood by the newly-made pulpit as he told the story of the glory of the Lord filling the temple of Solomon many centuries ago. The congregation then rose to its feet and answered the question posed by Daniel Aguilar.

"Do you give this building to God for Him to be worshipped here?"

And all the people said "*Hichuk*" (Amen).

"*This is the generation* [of Tzeltals] *that seek Thy face, O Lord!*"

...that the trial of your faith
...though it be tried by fire,
might be found unto praise
and honor
and glory.
I Peter 1:7

With each triumph
in the newly-created early church,
a corresponding trial arose
which threatened to intimidate
the new believers.

Chapter Eleven

Persecution

Though all were thrilled with the new freedom allowed them as children of the living God, they had ingrained in them from many years past a fear of the *shamans*. When they had defied tradition and refused to pay for the mass to St. Thomas for corn planting, they had aroused the fierce opposition of the town leaders who were determined to maintain power over the Tzeltals.

One morning early, we received official notice that we, with all the believers in Corralito, were to appear at the town hall at nine that morning. Since it was a four-hour journey, mostly uphill, there was no possibility of our arriving in time. We postponed our journey by one day, giving time for the word to spread all through the mountains that we were to appear before the town officials together.

At dawn the next day, the cowhorns signalled the beginning of our trip to Oxchuc. The first hour was made up of excited chatter; then, as the morning progressed, the Indians became increasingly more quiet as they became sobered by the seriousness of their situation. More than a hundred men and women converged on the town to defend themselves against what they knew was strong opposition. At the edge of town, we all gathered in a group for prayer. From the Book of Acts which we were translating at the time, they realized no new freedom comes without its price and the price for them was persecution. But they were well-armed.

In one hand Francisco, the group spokesman, held a Spanish Bible. In the other, he grasped a small, red-backed copy of the Mexican Constitution.

At the town hall, the town president and the somewhat inebriated town secretary found themselves confronted by a determined group of Tzeltals.

Francisco began their defense. "*Señor Presidente*, here is God's Book which tells what we believe. We believe every word in it because it is God's Word to us."

Neither the president nor the secretary could read Spanish and they had nothing to say in the face of such positive statements. Francisco held up his left hand.

"And here, *Señor*, is a copy of the law which says we have a right to believe as we do."

He opened the copy of the Mexican Constitution and pointed to Article 24 which was underlined.

Every person has the right to profess
whatever religion he pleases.

The two officials backed down somewhat shamefacedly. Their plot had backfired, for the day previous they had assembled three hundred irate townspeople, armed with rifles and *machetes* to confront the believers. The rumor had spread that the Christians planned to set fire to St. Thomas. An aroused populace had rallied to protect their patron saint. When only four young believers unaware of the plot, had inadvertently gone to Oxchuc that day, the townspeople had vented their wrath on them by mauling them, then putting them in jail. The four dauntless Christians with the persecution of first century Christians fresh in mind, had promptly given the Word of God to a fellow prisoner. When no other believers appeared that day, the mob dispersed, somewhat chagrined.

Martin Gourd's life was threatened again and again as the instigator of this new belief. The *shamans*, fearing their power over the people was permanently damaged, conspired with town officials to hang him from the rafters of the town hall. Juan Nich and his followers threatened to kill Martin and burn down his hut. Once again on his knees, Martin got out his victrola, opened his Bible and waited for his assassins. They never came.

Let those who put their trust in thee rejoice,...
because thou defendest them.

A scribbled note from a passing rancher warned Florence and me that a crowd from Oxchuc was plotting to set fire to our house. Each night, seventy or more of our faithful Indian friends gathered for prayer asking the Lord to "show Himself strong in their behalf." After the prayer meeting, most of them camped around our house for the night to protect us. Even some who had originally opposed our teaching began to give in when we were threatened because, they admitted,

"The believers haven't committed any crime and besides, they have God on their side!"

Over the trails tramped believers new to the faith themselves but eager to share the message with others. The victrolas were in constant use, giving forth the Gospel. The seed fell on fertile soil and yielded fruit a hundredfold.

As new ones turned to the Lord in ever-expanding areas, the list of those wanting to be legally married and thus become eligible to join the Christian congregation, grew.

The town secretary had performed one marriage in the entire previous year. When we approached him with a list of two hundred couples who wanted a legal ceremony, he was stunned. He also would not cooperate.

We tried another town. The authorities there demanded birth certificates which no Indian possessed, as well as an exorbitant fee which no one could pay.

We petitioned the governor of the State of Chiapas to authorize the mass marriage of all Indian couples who were willing to obey the law. No action.

I finally wrote to the head of the Department of Indian Affairs in Mexico City informing him that 225 Indian couples in the remote Chiapas mountains wanted to legalize their marriages. Unheard of!

But it brought a response. An official from the Department of Indian Affairs met us in Oxchuc. His glance went from the tribal elders dressed in ragged garments (some slightly drunk, most dirty, all showing signs of dissipation) then to the believers, clean, well-dressed and well-behaved.

Courteously, he listened to the complaints of the Oxchuc officials.

"*Señor patron*," the town secretary began, "We are distressed because these believers refuse to respect Santo Tomas any more. They won't give money for the *fiestas*."

Instead of sympathy from the official, they received a lecture on the evils of drink and dissipation. Some looked as if they wanted to slink away but the doorway was blocked by the believers.

With a gesture of his hand, the Delegate indicated the Christians.

"These others are free to believe the way they want. Our Constitution guarantees that right to 'evangélicos' and 'católicos' alike."

A date was set for processing the marriage forms. As we left, the town president took hold of my sleeve and whispered furtively,

"I want to come to your meetings as soon as I leave office. Will you pray for me, me'tik?"

Opposition came not only from the Indian religious leaders but from another source. The mestizo liquor dealers were not pleased with losing some of their best clients. In an underhanded scheme, they managed to have Juan Nich appointed town president. At the same time, the bishop and a delegation of priests began an all-out campaign to stamp out God's Word in Tzeltal.

In an effort to gain a few more converts, they offered to baptize all comers at a reduced rate. Propaganda accusing us of being deceivers was distributed throughout the Oxchuc region. Then a mob marched past our house with drums beating, red banners flying and cross held high, on their way to Abasolo where Juan Mucha had first heard the records. At the home of Pedro Santis, the first believer in that town, the procession paused long enough to rifle his house, tear up his hymnal and throw it in the fire.

Then without a written order or any explanation, they hauled Pedro and his son with two relatives, off to jail. The protesting neighbors were forbidden to accompany them.

The next day was Sunday. Just after the congregation had prayed fervently for their persecuted brethren to be released, in walked Pedro and the others, unharmed.

"Just like the Apostle Peter was released from jail by an angel when the whole church prayed for him," some said wonderingly. Even the name was right!

Pedro had been warned to leave Abasolo as his enemies planned to burn down his house. Instead, we sent off letters in two directions to government authorities. Eventually, they replied with the guarantee that the new believers were to be protected in Abasolo as well as the rest of Mexico. The Word of God continued to spread.

Harassment continued. One Sunday in February, halfway through the church service, we were handed an official message:

To arrange a matter of penal nature, you are ordered to appear before the Head of Indian Affairs of the State of Chiapas Tuesday at ten a.m.

Impossible! Las Casas was two days' journey from us by horseback! We had to scramble to find horses, get prepared and leave before daybreak on Monday morning. We never stopped for rest until late into the night. We slept by the trail on an open threshing floor, nearly frozen, then rode like Jehu to arrive on time.

At the stroke of ten, Florence and I walked calmly into the office of Indian Affairs, to present ourselves to the official who had summoned us. He handed us a document of numerous typewritten pages with multiple charges against us:

• Disturbing the peace in Oxchuc

• Building a large chapel without permission

• Fomenting opposition to local officials

• Dividing the Tzeltals into two warring factions.

Suspicious, I glanced quickly down the long list of signatures at the end of the document: the names were those of all the liquor dealers in the region!

"*Señor Licenciado,* I believe I can explain. These are the names of all the *mestizos* in the area who make a living selling liquor to the Indians illegally. Now that the Indians have heard the Word of God, they do not drink any more. This is really a protest of the liquor dealers against their losing their former clients!"

The *Licenciado* comprehended instantly. Part of his official responsibility was to stamp out illegal sale of liquor to the Indians. In reply to our accusers, he drew up a strong letter in which he refuted the charges against us and endorsed our work to "help end the drunkenness among the Oxchuc Tzeltals."

Exonerated, we gave the *Licenciado* a copy of our Tzeltal primer and Spanish-Tzeltal dictionary in token of our appreciation. When I came down with German measles the next day, we hoped I had not also given that to him!

Our little hut began to look like a small scale courtroom as Florence and I began to help the 225 couples who wished to become legally married begin the first stages of their marriage petitions. With four witnesses for each couple, we filled in their full names using the Spanish clan name rather than the picturesque Indian names of plants and animals they used more frequently. We guessed wildly at their ages as none of them knew this accurately. Since none of them could read and write, they nervously implanted their thumbprints on the marriage petitions. As president of Oxchuc, it was Juan Nich's duty to sign his name seven times to each one of the 225 marriage documents. Punishment enough for his animosity!

The plans for the Easter service were nearing completion. Since it was to be the first time most of the believers could appreciate what the resurrection meant, we had put our hearts and souls into planning a meaningful service. Whole groups of people had planned their special presentations of music. We had mimeographed four new hymns to distribute at the Easter service.

Suddenly late Wednesday night, one of our Indian neighbors burst into our home, tears streaming down his face. He shouted,

"The *templo* is on fire!"

We rushed outside to the awesome sight across the valley. Tongues of flame relentlessly licked the tinder-dry thatch of the roof. Even from that distance, ten minutes' walk away, we could hear the crackling and roaring of the blaze. Horrified, we watched as the roofpoles and rafters were enveloped in flames, crashing down inside the *templo*. For an hour, the fire raged. When it had burned itself out, only a gutted shell was left. As if from a burnt offering, a massive column of smoke rose in the windless night.

Tomás Kituk who lived nearby, had been the first to notice the fire. He had just returned home from helping us with the mimeographing of the new hymns when he noticed the far side of the *templo* roof was in flames. A malicious enemy had tossed a firebrand onto the dry thatch. Tomás shouted to waken others who came on the run from nearby huts. A fire in this area was a catastrophe and since it was dry season, it burned out of control. Some of the more courageous men climbed on the burning roof to try to put out the flames. Others braved flames and smoke to drag out the portable organ and seventy-six wooden benches. Others dislodged the large front door and one window with their *machetes*. Despite their frenzied efforts, the work of a hundred men for a full month was destroyed within an hour. The fine new chapel, pride of all the Corralito believers, was a charred ruin.

Then unbelievably, while the ruined *templo* was still smoldering, the firefighters knelt and prayed,

"Lord, forgive the ones who set fire to our *templo*. It is because they haven't believed on You that they did this."

We dared not leave the house alone for fear the same enemies might toss a burning firebrand onto our thatched roof also, and our precious portions of the Word would be lost to fire. While Florence was at the burning chapel encouraging the believers, I remained behind to pray with a heavy heart.

"Lord, don't let the fire that destroyed the *templo* also destroy the faith of these new believers."

About one in the morning, I heard voices coming nearer. Weary and smelling of smoke, the firefighters were on their way home with Juan Mucha in the lead. Undaunted by the loss, his first words to me were:

"God permitted the chapel to be set on fire so that our faith would be strengthened and His Word would spread all the more! Besides, it wasn't large enough for us all to get inside and we need to build a bigger one!"

Their faith had come through the fire "*as pure gold*."

Two days later, on Good Friday, believers congregated from all over the region for the service. First, they cleaned out the charred rubble and ashes. Then, they crowded inside the fire-gutted walls still partially standing, to hear God's Word. Somehow, the story of Christ's suffering had a deeper meaning than ever for we had been permitted to share in "*the fellowship of His sufferings.*"

Chief Marcos Ensin, who had never before stated his faith publicly, urged the congregation:

"Let us all believe on the Lord with one heart. Let us not become two-hearted about believing now that enemies of God have burned down our *templo,*" he counseled.

Easter Day the neighborhood cocks aroused us all at three-thirty a.m. to summon us for the sunrise service. Struggling against sleep, we dressed in our voluminous Indian skirts, embroidered *huipils* and strands of red beads.

We stepped outside. The still, blanket-covered forms on the ground were stirring and coming to life. With believers before and behind us, we crossed the valley in full moonlight and made our way up the trail to the *templo.* The roofless, fire-ravaged chapel was already full of hushed, reverent people. It was four-thirty a.m.

As the Angel had announced to the Lord's disciples that first Easter morn, the Indians began to sing,

He is alive, He is alive.
Christ Jesus has risen from the dead!

In the cool pre-dawn darkness, we forgot the fire-scarred walls surrounding us. We were only aware of the Lord's presence and of the presence of hundreds of our Indian brethren whose faith had been *"tried by fire."* Anew, we realized that the true *templo* consists not of a building but of believers in whose hearts *"Christ dwells by faith."*

MAP OF MEXICO
SHOWING CHIAPAS

MEXICO

CHIAPAS

Mexico, "Land of Enchantment"

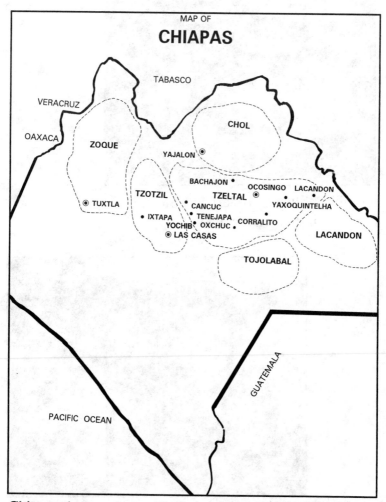

MAP OF
CHIAPAS

TABASCO

VERACRUZ

OAXACA

CHOL

ZOQUE

YAJALON ◎

BACHAJON •

⊙ TUXTLA

TZOTZIL

• OCOSINGO LACANDON
TZELTAL ◎

• CANCUC

YAXOQUINTELHA •

• IXTAPA

• TENEJAPA

• OXCHUC CORRALITO

YOCHIB •

LACANDON

◎ LAS CASAS

TOJOLABAL

GUATEMALA

PACIFIC OCEAN

Chiapas, home of many Indian tribes including the Tzeltal Indians who were co-workers, helpers and friends to Marianna and Florence.

Bill Bentley and Marianna Slocum
on their engagement day.

Professor Alfonso Villa and family
in front of Marianna's first home in Yochib.

Portrait of Martin Gourd
(Oil painting by Katherine Voigtlander)

Maria and Maruch

Dr. Eugene Nida of the American Bible Society
checking Scriptures with Martin and Marianna.

Florence
Gerdel, R.N.

Shepherds in the Christmas Pageant.

It was considered a great honor to portray the Wise Men in the Christmas Pageant. (L. to R.) Isidro Ensin, Tomas Ch'ijk and Marcos Ensin with Regina (Martin Gourd's daughter) and Juan Balte' as Mary and Joseph.

The building of the chapel at Corralito

Prayer before planting the cornfields

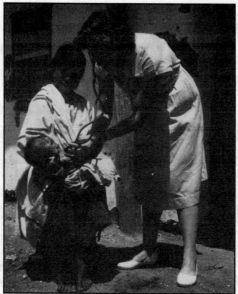

Mary Morison with a sick infant
at the Corralito clinic

Easter Sunday, 1957, in the burned-out *Templo*

Uncle Cam Townsend (Photo by Cornell Capa)

Marianna's parents, Stephen and Jeannette Slocum, hear
newly-literate Tomas Kituk read a Tzeltal Scripture.

Domingo Mendez' family shared
their hut with the translators.
(Photo by Cornell Capa)

Corralito Congregation
(Photo by Life photographer, Cornell Capa)

...in the place where it was said unto them,
"Ye are not My people,"
there shall they be called
the sons of the living God.
Romans 9:26

The resilience of the Indians
never failed to amaze me.

Though their labor of months
had literally gone up in smoke,
they were not discouraged.

Juan Mucha's undeviating faith
buoyed the rest of us
through this grave disappointment.

To the congregation
crowded into the roofless,
charred chapel that Easter morning,
he said,

"I willl build My church."

Chapter Twelve

"I Will Build My Church"

"If others think we are going to give up our faith because our chapel has been burned down, we will show them that we believe on the Lord more than ever."

He spoke for them all.

If weekly services were to continue, we needed a roof over our heads since six months of torrential rainy season were about to begin. The arrangements for the legal marriages of the believers were nearly completed and we needed a place for the ceremony. Something had to be done - and quickly.

Out of their poverty, barefooted Indians who could hardly spare any coin dug deep into their red sashes and pulled out almost all that they had for the rebuilding of the *templo*. In one offering, they gave 800 *pesos* in small change.

They reasoned, "After all, we gave ten *pesos* apiece for the church in Oxchuc before the Word of God came. Now with one heart, we give for the *templo* of the living God."

It took a great deal of organization and sacrificial work. This time, they decided not to give their enemies such easy opportunity. They would build with inflammable roofing material. The work was not without difficulties.

The nearest town where aluminum roofing could be purchased was two days away on foot. One hundred and fifty-seven sheets were borne on

willing backs over a rough trail. Long poles
needed to be dragged to the site for the framework.
Hammers and nails were a novelty to Indians accustomed to lashing their roofs together with
vines. Two missionaries from the Reformed
Church in America flew out to Corralito to help
their Indian brothers nail on the aluminum roofing. There was a tremendous spirit of cama-
raderie with this renewed project for every work
day produced more joy than a harvest festival.

When early in August it was completed, the
shiny new *templo* roof was more imposing than
ever for the sun caught its sheen and radiated for
miles around that here was the *Templo of the
Living God.*

Juan Nich, of course, was never idle. He accused Florence and me of threatening the Indians
"with brute force." When that accusation was
refuted at the District Attorney's office, he turned
to harassment of the believers. As town president
for a year, he forced twenty-five of the strongest
Christians to report to Oxchuc every Sunday for
military drill. In obedience to governmental authority, the men marched for several hours then
raced to Corralito in order to be present at part of
the service. They would arrive breathless but re-
joicing that they had been in time for some of the
singing!

Young Martin Ensin from Pakwina was a chief
target of Juan Nich. He had been born congenitally deformed with fingers missing from both
hands and his feet grotesquely askew at the
ankles. His active, inquisitive mind was ready for
the Gospel when Martin Gourd had presented it
to him a year or so earlier. At the time of his salvation, he held an elective office in the town

church. Martin Ensin immediately refused to
have anything more to do with idols or to attend
any more *fiestas*. In his official capacity as town
president, the infuriated Juan Nich hauled him
into town hall and tried to force him to recant. He
refused. When Juan Nich publicly boxed his ears
and slapped his face for being a hated Protestant,
he meekly submitted to this abuse. In God's
Word, he had read that he should "*turn the other
cheek.*"

The Ensin family turned, one by one, to God.
Old Grandmother Ensin with her patient face
crisscrossed with wrinkles, led the way. Chief
Marcos Ensin, a fine figure of a clan leader and
father of Martin, believed as did his lively sloe-eyed
daughters. The only one who refused to accept
the Lord was Marcos' younger brother, Isidro. He
had been the one to sign the lease on our Yochib
property many years before but he had never soft-
ened in his rejection of the Lord's message. Hard-
fisted and hard-drinking, he bragged that he
would never believe in God. Instead, he had com-
mandeered every able-bodied man in Oxchuc to
rebuild the town church and to contribute liberal-
ly to it. Their only alternative was to spend time
in jail. He had burned extra-long candles to Santo
Tomas, beseeching him to "get rid of the two *gringas* who were deceiving his townspeople."

One day, young Martin received a summons
from this same uncle. He debated about going for
Isidro had been drinking and was noted for his
violence as well as his opposition to the family's
newfound faith. Martin decided to take the risk.

Arriving at his uncle Isidro's house, he stepped
inside not knowing what he would face. There sat
Isidro, hunched against one wall of the hut, head
bowed, face contorted with pain. Martin gasped

in sympathy. Isidro was suffering from a dreaded eye disease that has blinded many Tzeltals. Wearily, without trying to open his inflamed eyes, Isidro motioned Martin to a low seat by the fire.

In a gruff voice, he ordered the young man, "Talk to God for me. Ask Him to make my eyes well."

Before Martin could clear his throat, Isidro changed his tone to plead, "I want to believe God's Word, too."

Martin was skeptical. His thoughts raced. What if his uncle's repentant attitude persisted only as long as the pain in his eyes lasted?

Isidro sensed his nephew's hesitation. "I have been thinking about turning my heart to God for a long time," he assured Martin. "I am going to believe with all my heart."

Martin's skepticism persisted. He questioned his uncle.

"Do you realize what it means to be a follower of the Lord? You can't get drunk any more. You can't be angry any more. You can't attend pagan *fiestas* any more. You have to let God change your heart completely."

Isidro was resolute. He instructed Martin,

"Take down that wooden cross I used to worship. Throw out all my incense-burners. Then kneel down and pray for me. I will believe in God."

It was not Martin who convinced Isidro he should believe in God. It was Isidro who persuaded Martin that he was in earnest about believing. The blackest sheep of the Ensin family had entered the fold!

God was faithful. In answer to the believers' prayers, He healed Isidro's eyes. The following Sunday, Isidro attended services in the *templo* for the first time with his two wives and children. They sat in the very front row to prove they were truly believers now!

The next day, he came to work on the new chapel being built in Pakwina. A skilled carpenter, Isidro had been healed just in time to help his brothers in the building of their own place of worship for Corralito was four hours' journey away. The congregation had grown so large there and the distance was so great that Christians in distant settlements were beginning to build their own local chapels. Because of Isidro's skill, the roof on the Pakwina *templo* was constructed with pegged wooden shingles setting it off very distinctively. It also had six clear windows in the sides, a feature none of the believers' huts possessed.

As the Tzeltals became aware of their "heavenly citizenship", their sense of earthly worth increased. Accustomed as they had been to being considered "dogs" by the *mestizos*, they underwent a revolution in their own thinking of their place in the society to which they belonged. They developed a strong desire to become "respectable" in the eyes of their fellow Christians. Those whose loyalties had been limited to their own kinship groups and tribal area became aware for the first time, of their citizenship in the nation of Mexico.

More and more couples came to us at Corralito, requesting their names be included in the marriage ceremony which would make their marriages legal and enable them to become full-fledged members of their congregations. We sensed that the legal ceremony would give a dignity and a stability to marriage which it had not had under tribal rules. It would deal a deathblow to such tribal customs as child marriages and plural wives. A precedent would be set which the whole Tzeltal tribe would follow. From now on, Tzeltal Christians would ask for a wife in the traditional way and pay for her with the customary gifts with the exception of liquor. The actual marriages would take place before proper civil authorities instead of the old men of the clan and would be legally binding as no tribal marriage rites had been.

Pursuing one devious method after another, the opposition to Christians continued. One week before the civil judge was to come to Corralito, the heads of all the families in Corralito were summoned to Oxchuc by the Department of Indian Affairs. Waving a paper in front of the bewildered Indians, the officials asked,

"Did you sign this document?"

The officials displayed a typewritten paper demanding the removal of the *gringas*, signed with the names and fingerprints of all the Indian believers. Dumbfounded, the Christians remembered that the *mestizo* schoolteacher in Corralito had borrowed a typewriter and typing paper from us and typed out a letter to which he had obliged them all to affix their fingerprints. None of them had known what the document said.

Heartily, they protested,

"We invited our sisters to live in Corralito and we want them to stay there. They give us medicine, teach us to read and tell us God's Word."

The Lord's prophetic words were fulfilled,

You shall be called before rulers for My sake...
The case was dismissed.

Excitement mounted as the day for the marriages drew near. Three generations of the Mucha family would be getting married the same day - greying Grandfather Mucha, his son, Alonzo, and his grandson, Juan.

Former *shaman*, Tomás, put his thumbprint on the official-looking document with his wife, Maria, coyly adding hers to his.

Chief Marcos Ensin affixed his signature with a flourish, explaining to an impressed audience the importance of legal marriage.

In their eagerness to participate in the ceremony with everyone else, some of the younger generation began to look around for wives so they could join in, too!

It was a time of great seriousness for some had to face the decision of whether to be obedient and send back their second wives or to keep them and not be obedient. Some made one decision, some another. They could not be members of the congregation if they had more than one wife.

August 6, 1951. A day eagerly anticipated.

Up before dawn, the Corralito Christians worked feverishly to prepare for their Wedding Day. The chapel, newly refurbished with fresh plaster, glass windows and the large front door which had been rescued from the fire, was a tribute to the Lord they loved and served.

Each couple had paid a five-*peso* marriage fee then contributed an additional two *pesos* toward the cows which were slaughtered for fresh meat for the lavish feast they had prepared. The women had decorated the long thatched-roofed hut next door with streamers in red, white and green, Mexico's national colors. Reeds lashed together with vines provided dining tables and poles laid across forked sticks provided seats for the diners.

When we suggested a wedding picture with the couples standing together instead of the men on one side and the women on another, we upset traditional tribal etiquette. With some embarrassed giggling, they complied, many with children also included in their wedding photo.

We had been anticipating the civil judge who was to perform the legal ceremony all morning. He had not arrived. Florence rushed back to the house to place a radio call by our two-way radio transmitter to the Missionary Aviation Fellowship pilot, E.W. Hatcher ("Hatch"), to see if he could help with the transportation of the judge. Hatch was off the ground to pick up the judge and fly him out to the ranch before Florence had completed the call.

Shortly before three that afternoon, we heard the little plane flying overhead to let us know the judge was on his way. It would be another two and a half hours by horseback after he landed at the nearest airstrip (on a Mexican ranch with the only level ground for miles around) before he could reach Corralito.

Don Abelino, who had gone to the airstrip ahead of time with horses to meet the judge, told us afterwards that the judge had been filled with trepidation as they circled overhead and saw such a huge congregation of Indians milling around. He had never seen so many Indians in one place who were not involved in heavy drinking and brawling and he wondered if it were safe for him!

It was nearly dark by the time the judge and don Abelino arrived on horseback. The couples were seated side by side in self-conscious solemnity with their heads bowed in prayer when the still-apprehensive judge stepped inside the chapel. The light from two gasoline lanterns highlighted the awed, intent faces of 225 couples about to be united in holy matrimony.

The judge's nervousness turned to whole-hearted enthusiasm. He sensed the significance of this rite for the all-Indian community - their first collective attempt to comply with the law of Mexico. Taking a deep breath, he launched into a full and lengthy explanation of all the advantages as well as all the obligations which resulted from legal marriage. He sounded like an evangelical preacher!

• A wife could not run off to her parents' hut to aggravate her husband.

• A husband couldn't send back his wife merely because she didn't mix his corn gruel on time.

• Parents were not free to take their daughter away from their son-in-law on the slightest pretext such as failure to visit them.

• Children were not to be given in marriage until they were of legal age - a much-debated point among Indians who did not know their exact ages and who were accustomed to marrying off their children at a tender age so they could "grow up together."

• In a society which granted women almost no rights at all, women who were legally married would have rights to their children as well as to their husband's property. Oxchuc customs were never the same again.

The judge read out the names of each couple to be married, all 225 of them. Solemnly, he raised his arm and declared in the name of the law, that all those standing before him were legally united

in marriage. Near the judge stood Chief Marcos
Ensin, tears of pride running down his weathered
cheeks as he and his people together complied
with the law of their country.

After the long ceremony had ended, the
"newlyweds" filed out of the front benches of the
templo. Some of the younger ones who actually
were bride and groom, held hands in the darkness
in a further breach of tribal etiquette. Scurrying
across the clearing to take their places at the long
tables in the specially-decorated hut, they eventually each found places. First, they bowed their
heads, as thanks was offered to the Lord for the
feast. Steaming bowls of meat and a few candies
were set before them. This was **their wedding** and
they were determined to enjoy it to the fullest!
Their relatives and friends squatted around
campfires in the clearing to sing and to share the
fresh meat.

We sat with the judge in one corner of the
decorated hut, watching the festive joy of the
throng of Indians, aware of muted, contented
voices on all sides of us.

"What did you do to these Indians to make them
into law-abiding citizens?" he wondered. "I can
remember when it was dangerous to even venture
into their territory!"

We told him of the life-changing effect the Lord's
Word had produced in these hungry Indian
hearts. He was awestruck.

Humble Indian leaders, untaught by men's
standards but Spirit-taught from God's Word,
realized that the Tzeltal Church must be built
upon the foundation of vital, individual faith in the
Lord Jesus Christ. Though the marriage ceremony
had been a mass affair, baptism into the Church

of Jesus Christ was a deeply personal, serious matter. Don Daniel would have been willing to perform the baptismal rites on all who professed to believe but Juan Mucha insisted on much more exacting standards. He quoted James,

It is useless
to say that you have heart-obedience,
if your life doesn't show it,
if your conduct does not verify it.

He had helped translate this just days before. The caliber of the future Tzeltal Church owed much to this decision of its Spirit-led leader based on the newly-translated Word.

With several hundred candidates on the list for baptism, the Indian leaders began their questioning. I sat nearby to lend support as well as to discover how effectively the Word of God had been "translated" into Indian hearts. Each couple took their seats nervously facing Juan as he asked,

"Do you know where God is?"

"Yes, He is in heaven, not in a niche in the town church."

"Do you know who obtained your salvation, and how?"

"Yes, we were bought with a great price, by Christ on the cross."

"Do you know what would have been your fate if Christ had not paid for your sins?"

"Yes, we would have had to pay for our own sins and we would be lost eternally."

Most had learned their lessons well for they knew in whom they believed.

Then Juan's penetrating questions proceeded to query the outward evidence of an inward faith.

"Do you still get angry?" he asked, in the belief that a change of disposition was the surest sign of a change of heart.

"Do you pray any oftener than when you drink your corn gruel and when you come to services?" He wanted to determine how vital a part prayer played in their daily lives.

Then he wanted to know, "Do you still attend pagan *fiestas*?" The answer indicated how far the old life had been replaced by the new.

"Are you of one heart with your wife...your husband?" Family relationships were of utmost importance to the Christians.

Finally, he asked evidence of what is the surest characteristic of a child of God: "Do you love all of your fellow-Christians?"

None weak in their faith could get past that battery of questions. More than a third of the candidates for baptism were encouraged to "believe more fully" and were postponed.

The Lord set His seal on the decisions made during those days. With few exceptions, those who were accepted for baptism remained true to the Lord. Those whose baptism was postponed, searched their hearts and took a more definite stand for the Lord.

"A morning without clouds" dawned on August 12, 1951, one of the most precious days in all our years of service for we saw the beginnings of the harvest God had so richly provided. One hundred sixty-two believers, candidates for baptism and church membership, were ushered into the front benches of the *templo*. Dressed in their best Indian garb, they presented a colorful picture. Some of the women wore brightly-colored ribbons entwined in their sleek black braids. The men had smoothed down their unruly hair for the occasion. An arch of palms and flame-colored bougainvillea decorated the platform for the baptismal rites.

Subdued by the momentous solemnity of the event, an expectant hush fell over the entire *templo* of believers as don Daniel began the service. This was the day the Tzeltal Church would officially come into being.

The candidates for baptism stood before all their brethren to reply to the questions proffered by don Daniel. As he spoke in Spanish, I translated into Tzeltal but the believers were so eager to assert their new faith that they didn't wait for me to finish before they spoke up with the answers! Then as their names were read, they came up to the platform and knelt on a straw mat beneath the arch. The minister said in Tzeltal so that all could understand:

I baptize you in the name of God the Father, God the Son, and God the Holy Spirit.

As the minister laid his hand on each bowed head in baptism, they prayed silently. Juan, the "*beloved disciple,*" and his equally-devoted wife Maria were the first to be baptized. Then other married couples, some widows and several teenagers, until all one hundred sixty-two had been baptized. As they knelt, a shaft of sunlight from the row of windows high above the platform rested on their bowed heads like a divine benediction. They had "*confessed Christ before men.*" They had the assurance of His Word that He would "*confess them before His Father in heaven.*"

To my parents, whose faithful prayers had followed me through all the struggles of establishing Christ's kingdom among the Tzeltals, I wrote,

In answer to a year or more of prayer, we have seen the Lord bring into being the Tzeltal Church! I know you will magnify the Lord with me for all the blessing poured out here that your prayers have brought to pass.

The Lord is good,
a stronghold in the day of trouble,
and He knoweth those who trust in Him.
Nahum 1:7

With the growth of the Tzeltal churches
came desperate needs -

those of literacy,
those of medicine,
those of ready access to supplies
and transportation.

It sometimes seemed
the more we accomplished,
the more there was to be done.

Chapter Thirteen

Growing Needs

One evening as I was checking another portion of Scripture with some of the more earnest Indians, they began to question me.

"*Me'tik*, how long will it take you to finish translating the whole New Testament for us?"

I picked up the Spanish Bible we were working from and showed them how many pages there were in the New Testament. All but a few pages had been translated into Tzeltal in the first draft.

One bright fellow noticed for the first time that the Bible contained an Old Testament as well as a New, and that the Old Testament contained even more pages than the New Testament!

"How long will it take you to translate the Old Testament into our language, too? We want all of God's Book!" they insisted.

One picked up a book of devotional readings and added, "We want this in our language, too!"

Another pointed to a thick volume of Jamieson, Fausset and Brown's Commentary on the Bible, one of many I used frequently for consultation.

"You must translate this for us, too!"

My life's work was cut out for me. Newly-awakened, newly-literate Indians wanted books. But the only book most of them would ever own would be God's Book.

More Indian Christians had to be taught to read so that they would be "readers" of the Word and

not "hearers" only. The coming of God's Word had
given the Tzeltals an incentive for learning to read:
they wanted to know for themselves what God
said. Now that they were free from the fear of
being cursed if they learned to read, they had a
purpose in becoming literate and they were not
afraid to attempt it.

We taught some of the believers to read in-
dividually. Others were taught the primers in
classes and still others taught one another. The
young leader of one of the outlying chapels came
to our house with a week's supply of corn gruel,
determined to learn to read before he returned
home. By poring over the first primer night and
day for a week, he was able to read it haltingly by
the time his corn was gone.

Another discovered a sudden thirst for learning
when he found out the girl he wanted to marry was
making good progress in the first primer. Long
after everyone else had gone home, we could hear
him out on the porch reading the syllables by the
light of his flashlight: *ta, te, ti, to, tu.*

An older man brought his primer to us to show
us how much he had learned. He proudly repeated a whole page to us from memory with his
primer closed!

It was harder for some than for others. One
pupil we despaired of ever teaching to read. By
dint of perseverance and prayer, Miguel not only
learned to read but also became a preacher.

A new status-symbol now existed among our
Tzeltal brethren: a printed portion of God's Word,
lovingly enfolded in a new bandana kerchief and
carried everywhere by its owner.

And as the New Testament neared completion, the Lord opened another door to further

implement the spread of His Word. I received a letter from a distinguished Mexican anthropologist, Dr. Aguirre Beltran, of the National Indian Institute. The government of Mexico was planning an extensive reading campaign among the Tzeltals and Tzotzils in their own languages and wanted our cooperation as linguistic consultants!

Upon seeing the literacy materials we had prepared in Tzeltal, he immediately ordered twelve hundred copies of each of the Tzeltal primers and requested me to teach fifteen Indian teachers from all parts of the tribe to use them and to teach others. Previous to this, the government educational policy had been to use only Spanish in their schools in the vain hope that Indian children might be able to pick up enough Spanish to become integrated into Mexican life. It had not worked.

Now, in the first full-scale literacy effort among the Indian population of Chiapas, the government was sponsoring the use of the Indian language and preparing Indian teachers to teach it. Having the government undertake literacy campaigns in the Indian tongues was a giant step toward "hastening God's Word" to every Indian tribe in Mexico.

I began my teaching assignment with fifteen students, some Christians whom I had recommended and a few others. Two from Yochib were Juan Nich and one of his henchmen! I had many opportunities that month to put into practice the Lord's admonition, "*Love your enemies.*" Juan Nich was insolent in class, muttering under his breath to undermine my instruction, distracting at every opportunity. Yet, he was careful not to be quite unruly enough to be dismissed from class as he wanted the job of teacher. The government was paying its *promotores* well!

When their one month of rudimentary "teachers' training" was over, the newly-appointed Indian teachers started off for different areas of the highland Tzeltals to build schools and to gather pupils together to be taught to read in Tzeltal. There were sixteen government schools and two literacy centers using the Tzeltal primers, teaching an estimated one thousand Indians to read in Tzeltal. The number of readers would determine the number of New Testaments the American Bible Society would print.

From areas where there were believers but no government schools, delegations came begging us to send them teachers, too.

"We want our children to be able to read God's Word, even if we are too old to learn ourselves," pled the parents.

Some of the believers, not trained at the government school, began evangelical schools for children where there were none.

Wycliffe sent out two new members to conduct a reading campaign. When these young women landed at the cattle ranch two and a half hours beyond Corralito, they found their trail led through the town of Abasolo. This was where Martin Gourd had first played the Gospel Recordings to Juan Mucha and family, but no converts from that dialect had ever been made. The villagers were in the midst of a *fiesta* and as soon as they saw two unfamiliar *gringas* passing through, they picked up sticks and stones and pelted the defenseless party with them. Some of the missiles found their mark.

Two days later, I landed at the same ranch airstrip when I returned from Las Casas. The plane's propellers had barely stopped turning before I was surrounded by worried believers from Corralito. They had come to warn me.

"*Me'tik*, the townspeople in Abasolo plan to waylay you. They want to put you in jail when you pass through their town!"

The *fiesta*-goers had been drinking heavily and we could expect trouble.

The two sons of the ranch owner heard of the planned ambush and offered to accompany us on their horses.

Single file, we started over the well-beaten path with those on foot leading and we three on horseback at the rear. At a turn in the trail, we caught a glimpse through the low underbrush of the massive masonry church dominating the squalid huts of the town. Ominously, the one cobblestone street of the town was nearly deserted except for some garrulous drunks lounging in front of the town hall. We had to pass them.

Just as the young man in the lead came even with them, several of the drunken men lunged toward him, pinned his arms to his side and shoved him bodily, cargo and all, into the smelly barred jail. The two ranchmen riding behind me spurred their horses to a gallop, swung themselves out of the saddle in front of the town hall and pulled the young man out of jail as unceremoniously as he had been shoved in. Outmaneuvered, the drunken crowd took to their heels, except for one who brashly grabbed the reins of my horse.

"Get off!" he insisted menacingly, as he tugged ineffectually at the reins and at my leg. I decided staying in the saddle was the better part of valor.

Frustrated, my antagonist renewed his threats, trying to focus on my face under a floppy hat brim.

Within a second, his head hit the cobblestone paving with a resounding crack as one of the ranchers spun him around and felled him with a well-placed blow on the jaw.

"Ride on ahead and have the Indian brethren follow you," the rancher advised. "There won't be any more trouble from these fellows."

I dug my heels into the horse's flanks and in a solid group, we hustled through town.

I knew how Moses felt, leading his people through the Red Sea with attackers on their heels!

The two incidents, one on top of the other, forced us to realize the necessity of having an airstrip nearer Corralito. It was not safe to bring our visitors through hostile territory.

We had used the airstrip on the cattle ranch for two years. Now, with the increased need for transportation in and out of Corralito, consultations with National Indian Institute officials in Las Casas and mounting supplies of medicines, primers and portions of Scriptures to be flown out to us, we knew we needed an airstrip close by. The believers had wanted us to have the little yellow airplane Hatch flew arrive in their territory almost from the beginning. But the problem was finding enough level land for an airplane to land and take off. Our terrain was mountainous, every feasible spot having been farmed for generations.

Two brothers whose land was less than a half hour's walk from Corralito, urged us to use their land. It was the best we could find and even then, it was not very level. Wedged in between two hills, it posed some very real problems even to the skilled pilot. At one end, the land dropped away abruptly; at the other end, a rushing stream coursed across the strip. Little hills blocked the entrance to the airstrip. The pilot would have to snake his way around these hills, come in at right angles to the strip, then turn suddenly, skip over the stream and set the plane down in less than one thousand feet. We never ceased to marvel at the fearlessness of the Missionary Aviation Fellowship pilots who agreed to land there. Through the years, many lives were saved because of their courage. With their help, the task of giving God's Word to the Tzeltals was accelerated.

The greatest immediate delight to having the airstrip convenient to us, though, was the visit by my own family: Mother, fragile from her illness, Dad and my brother Steve with his new wife, Donna. There was great excitement among all the Corralito believers that day! My family was their family! As Dad emerged from the plane, he greeted many of the Christians by name, clasping their hands with the warmth of many years' friendship. He recognized them from the photos I had sent home!

"Hello, Juan. God bless you, Domingo. How are you, Tomás?"

Mother had to be carried in a chair on an Indian's back for she had no strength to walk.

They were both in their seventies. The Indians had never seen white hair and were fascinated by my parents' generous supply. They would reach out and pat either of them on the head in affection.

Little babies were handed to Mother to hold as the Tzeltal mothers earnestly begged her to "talk to God" for them. There was no language barrier even though my parents spoke not a word of Tzeltal and the Indians not a word of English. Gifts of eggs and beans were brought to keep them from being hungry. Steve and Donna provided much interest, as well. It was a precious four days for all of us and served to make real to my family all the personalities and events I had written to them about for so many years.

Like Simeon, my father concluded the visit by saying,

Lord, now let thy servant depart in peace, according to thy word for my eyes have seen thy salvation which you have prepared before the face of all people. A light to lighten the Gentiles and the glory of thy people Israel.

Measles! The word strikes terror to any medical personnel working among Indians. They have no immunity to the disease and what might pass in America as a "routine childhood illness" proved to be a life-threatening disaster to the Tzeltals.

That spring, we had 550 cases of measles among our own acquaintances alone! The epidemic ravaged the entire area for many months. Time and again, Florence used up all her penicillin and sulfa pills, the only medicines of any use in combatting the devastating aftereffects of measles. Desperately ill patients crowded around the open half door of the little mud-walled clinic. Others were strewn on the hard ground outside the clinic with matted rags stuffed under their heads for pillows and threadbare blankets laid over their wasted bodies. Nearby squatted anxious relatives, patiently waiting for Florence to find a free moment to tend to them.

She looked over her diminished stock of medicine.

Then, she prayed in near desperation, "Lord, what shall I give this horde of sick people who will die without help?"

Immediately came the reassuring drone of a small plane. It was the little yellow MAF plane loaded with fresh supplies of antibiotics. "*Help from on high*" was not a thing of the past!

Day after day, critically ill Indians were carried up to the clinic. With no resistance to the disease and weakened by parasites and poor diet, adults as well as children fell prey to measles. Whole households were laid low, with no one well enough to fix food for the rest. Mounds of human misery lay on the ground outside our house and clinic, sick unto death. Many had the serious complications of pneumonia, bloody diarrhea, encephalitis and blindness. Florence battled against the epidemic with antibiotics and prayer. With no help but mine, she cared for 550 cases that spring. In spite of all she could do, thirty died. Compared to others who did not seek help, that was a low percentage.

The Indians had always blamed every illness on a curse placed on them by some enemy. Consequently, many revenge killings occurred when an epidemic struck. One of the worst *shamans* in the region was waylaid on the trail and brutally murdered, accused of casting the sickness that had decimated whole households. But among the Christian believers, not a single revenge killing took place! They were grief-stricken at losing their loved ones but they knew their Sovereign God was still in control!

Easter, the "Coming Alive", was a mystical time to the Indians. It was the time when "the earth dies and becomes new." Before we had brought the Gospel to Corralito, the most religious of the Tzeltals had offered special prayers before the crude handhewn cross which dominated the altar in their huts. On Good Friday, a large wooden image of Christ was taken out of its coffin-like case and fastened on a cross inside the church. All the other images were blindfolded as a sign of sorrow at the suffering of the Lord. An effigy of Judas was made, insulted and finally set on fire. On Saturday, the blindfolds were removed, the image of Christ replaced in his box and the crowd celebrated the renewal of the earth by unrestrained drinking and carousing.

Now that many Oxchuc Tzeltals worshipped a living Savior instead of a dead image, they wanted to gather together to praise Him on Easter Day. The Christian celebration of Easter (which replaced the former pagan observance) became a high point in the lives of Indian believers throughout the tribe. In spite of the measles epidemic, Indian evangelists traveled four days on foot to remote areas of the tribe to hold Easter services, some leaving children behind who were still suffering from the illness.

"I will put them into God's hands. He will care for them as I care for His work," one said. God answered his prayer.

Even though we did not encourage Indian Christians from other places to come to Corralito for Easter services for fear of spreading the epidemic even farther, more than a thousand were present during the three days of special services. Some families walked for a day to get to Corralito from far parts of the region. They swarmed over the trails leading to the *templo*, bringing fan-like palms, exotic pink blossoms and fragrant pine needles to decorate the chapel.

On Good Friday, the throng surged inside, packing the benches tightly, filling up the aisles with many peering in at the doors and windows. Many new faces were among them. Juan narrated from memory the entire story of the Last Supper, Jesus' trial and crucifixion, using the flannelgraph to illustrate. He missed not a single detail for it was indelibly engraved on his heart. Some, with their new portions of the Gospel, marked parts that meant the most to them. Others, whose eyes were dim with age or impaired by disease, stood up and strained to see the figures on the flannelgraph board. Some were hearing of Calvary love for the first time.

Among the audience was a couple who had taken their baby from one *shaman* to the next for healing and had finally brought him to Florence for prayer and medicine. The child recovered and the parents believed on the Lord. A blind daughter had brought her father to the service where he accepted the Lord. Two men were there who had accused a former *shaman* of casting curses on their children. He, in turn, had gone to their huts and explained the Word of God to them and prayed for the sick children. They recovered and the fathers decided to believe in God, also. Our eyes filled with tears as they traveled across the crowd of hundreds of Indians for each had a story to tell of a journey from gross superstition to joyful liberation.

Long before dawn on Easter morning, we heard singing in the *templo* across the valley. Words of praise welled up from hundreds of hearts:

Christ arose, released from death,
He defeated death, He defeated the grave,
He defeated Satan, He is Victor.

In the past weeks, almost every family had gone through the throes of serious illness. Some had passed through the valley of death. All had known fear all of their lives. Now they joined other believers, some for their first Easter, in praising their Risen Lord. By fire, by persecution, by suffering, the Lord was purifying the faith of "*a people for His name.*"

Call unto Me, and I will answer thee,
and show thee great and mighty things
which thou knowest not.
                              Jeremiah 33:3

It had been a long day.

Juan stretched his shoulders
to give them some relaxation.

He had preached for over an hour
on the first chapter of I Peter.

Then, he had taught a Sunday School class
for another hour.

Now, Juan and the elders
faced another long session -
this one called the "aiyej"
or "matters to be arranged."

Chapter Fourteen

Problems

We had sometimes wondered if I Peter were written especially for the Corralito Christians so pertinent to their lives was it. The singing had taken up nearly three hours. The believers began drifting homeward in order to get there before dark.

Juan, as unofficial pastor of the church at Corralito, found his wisdom and counseling skills tested severely from one Sunday to the next. As the believers faced the everyday problems of human relationships, they discovered they had another standard to live by - the Word of God. Everything was submitted to the arbitration of Juan and the other elders. Some of the problems were weighty and others were only those which would arise in the normal flow of family living. But they had to talk it over! Since Juan translated the Word into Tzeltal and understood his own people better than Florence or I, we left all discipline up to him and the elders. Florence usually had to tend to the sick after service but I sat in on the sessions as a silent observer, praying for the right decisions or solutions.

A little girl with an angry temper was brought to Juan for correction. He read to her from Ephesians 4:26,

When you get mad, don't get into sin by it. Don't still be angry when the sun goes down.

Three families did not want their sons to attend the government school in Las Casas because they feared the youngsters would "lose God's Word out of their hearts." The elders agreed that there was great risk in the city and it was more important for the boys to follow the Lord than to receive government schooling. They were advised to enroll their sons in one of the Christian schools where their young minds would be protected from the entanglements of non-Christian ideas.

A disobedient girl who ran away from home to the hut of other believers was advised to "*obey her parents in the Lord, for this is right.*" Her parents were instructed not to exasperate their daughter and to forgive her, treating her with kindness and compassion.

A wife whose husband had turned from the Lord and now threatened to cast her out unless she also turned, was told, "*He will believe when he sees your right behavior.*"

A Christian teacher at one of the outlying schools complained that some of the believers were not cooperating wholeheartedly with him. Juan read to them from I Peter, a passage we had just finished translating,

Be of one heart with one another, care about one another, feel for each other's trials, love as brothers, speak well with one another.

Thirty men were ordered by the town president of Oxchuc to work on the telegraph line against their will. Juan told them, "*Everyone ought to obey the authorities they are responsible to because it is God Who has made them authorities. It is by God's command that there are authorities.*"

A believer who was put out of his home by an unbelieving Mexican landowner found comfort in the assurance that he was "*considered worthy to suffer for Christ's sake.*" Here the kinship network took over and any believers with the same clan name as the persecuted one, would be expected to offer him shelter and food until the Lord provided something else for him and his family.

Widows were particular targets for the greed of unchristian men who wanted to take their land from them. Sometimes a small parcel of land for corn would be all she owned to keep her from starving and the avarice of her neighbors never failed to arouse my indignation. From the Scriptures, the Christians knew they were to "*take care of the widows and orphans*" but when the case involved a non-Christian, it occasionally had to be remanded to the town officials in Oxchuc. These men were not necessarily above accepting a bribe of liquor and the elders were rarely satisfied with the justice found there.

When money was requested by church officials in Oxchuc, Juan and the elders insisted they no longer were under obligation to false gods. The Constitution of Mexico guaranteed them the right to worship as they pleased and to contribute their money as they felt right.

Discipline was left entirely to the elders who set up even more rigid standards than I would have. Drunkenness, looked upon as a return to the old ways, was punished by a long period of being denied entry to the *templo* itself. The offenders could stand outside and listen but until the elders felt they had showed true repentance and were willing to confess before all the church, they were not allowed within the walls of the chapel. Every Sunday we had many "miscreants" milling about outside, peering into the windows wistfully but not allowed to enter. In cases of gross misconduct such as adultery, they were no longer called *hermano* or *hermana* (brother, sister) and did not receive a handshake from their fellow Christians. But always, no matter what the offense, the elders "talked to God" with anyone they counseled.

Family life among the Tzeltals was transformed. Conduct was now ordered by what God said. Parents who had previously been inclined to actual child abuse in the rearing of their little ones, were taught the principles of gentle rebuke in love. Men who had been free to conduct illicit affairs outside the marriage bond, were now held to fidelity to one wife alone. Women who had neglected their family duties, now realized the responsibilities they held as hub of the family.

There were other changes as families who had once been isolated on lonely hillsides now came into contact with one another. The Christian family took precedence over natural kinship ties and was more supportive. Previously, Tzeltals were rarely called by their own name but referred to by kinship terms such as "cousin," "father-in-law" or "uncle." Now the general term *hermano* or *hermana* gently reminded them of the new relationship we all bore in Christ.

Matters of propriety sometimes amused us. As boys and girls learned to read and write, they did what we would have considered quite natural - they wrote notes to one another. This was not a light matter to the church elders who sensed what could occur once a boy and girl began communicating without the approval of their parents! Many a youngster was called before the elders and reproved for flirtation!

Men and women sat on opposite sides of the chapel. The mingling of the sexes might prove too distracting! But there was a new freedom in the Christian congregation. Previous custom had forbidden a woman to speak directly to a man not her husband or close relative. To prove she was not trying to attract a male neighbor, a woman would use a falsetto voice and keep her eyes downcast when it was necessary to speak to him. With Christianity, the barriers were down and men and women could speak, looking one another directly in the eyes.

Not only were family relationships improved but economic betterment inevitably followed. When money was no longer spent on liquor, it could be used for purchasing sturdier clothes, more meat in the diet, the acquisition of horses and cattle, the whitewashing of dark huts.

In an article entitled "Cultural Changes Among the Oxchuc Tzeltals" (Estudios Antropológicos, 1956), I wrote,

Freedom from the galling debts incurred for liquor in its former multitudinous uses in their culture, and personal freedom from domination by alcoholism, engendered in the Tzeltals a new sense of self-respect. Public opinion, formed by the predominantly evangelical population, is now opposed to alcoholism, and the resulting social pressure is affecting even the non-Christian element in the region.

A second major change in the culture pattern of the Oxchuc Tzeltals has been the decline of witchcraft. Social control was formerly exercised in an unofficial but thoroughly effective way by "shamans" who claimed supernatural powers owing to their possession of a "nagual," in the form of a bird or animal, which enabled them to bring sickness or death upon anyone who departed from the norms of the indigenous culture.... As a result, the "shamans" ruled by instigating fear in the inhabitants of the whole region.

Among the indigenous evangelical community, this situation has now radically changed. Social control has passed from the hands of the older, illiterate, greatly-feared "shamans" into the hands of the young, literate, progressive leaders of the evangelical movement.... It is the young Christian leaders who set the high moral tone of the evangelical community by applying the precepts of Christian ethics to their own culture. There has been a resultant breakdown of the control formerly exercised by the "shamans," as many of them have abandoned their magical practices and others who were formerly under the "shamans'" domination have now asserted their independence in thought and deed.

The number of murders decreased for they had either been linked directly to the amount of liquor consumed or to vengeance killings for supposed curses brought on by witchcraft.

Even the Head of the Department of Indian Affairs in Chiapas remarked:

The notable change for the better among the Oxchucs is to be highly commended. Would that the same phenomenon would take place among every indigenous group in the land!

In addition to the changes brought about by Christian standards of living, there were the changes produced by the ready availability of medical assistance. Our facilities were meager indeed by Stateside standards but, with the addition of prayer, they were extremely effective. Miracles were expected and miracles were performed. The faith of these new believers was rewarded and our own increased as we saw God restore many critically ill babies to parents who previously had watched in hopeless grief as one or two or three of their children succumbed to similar illnesses.

One of the brothers who had given the land for the airstrip related one day,

When my child was sick some time ago, I wanted to do everything I could to make him well. The "shaman" tied me by my hands to the rafters of the house and beat me many times with a leather strap so I would confess whatever I might have done that had resulted in the sickness being cast upon the baby. But I hadn't done anything. It was all in vain. The baby died anyway and I still owe $120 for liquor I bought to pay him.

The new Christians expected older people to be healed as well. When old Alvina became acutely ill with a bronchial infection, thirty-two believers gathered at her house after a Sunday service to pray for her.

"She'll get well," Domingo Mucha stated without outward concern. "God answers prayer." He did.

The believers had almost a nonchalant attitude when I became very ill. I thought I was sick enough to die but they reasoned, "We still do not have all of God's Word yet so *Me'tik* will get well." Again, they were right.

Jacinto and Magdala were another couple in whom the Lord performed some true miracles, both spiritual and physical. Jacinto had no problem in yielding his heart to Christ but Magdala held on to the old ways in her heart. When their two little girls were suffering from the paroxysms of whooping cough, Magdala took them to Florence at the clinic for medicine. On the way back, the baby lost her breath in a bad coughing spell and turned an ashen gray.

"She's dead! My baby is dead!" wailed Magdala, rushing into their little hut at the top of a steep hill.

Jacinto refused to believe the baby had died. Falling to his knees, he said to Magdala,

"No, we're not going to let the devil have his way. We're not in his hands any more. We're going to pray to God."

Both parents knelt and earnestly beseeched God to spare their little one. She soon recovered from the convulsive seizure.

A few months later, Jacinto noticed their older child Rosa was not eating. When she began to whimper restlessly at night, they discovered a peculiar large hard swelling on one of her shoulders and another in the lower left side of her abdomen. Though the swellings were painful, they could not be drained like an abscess. Jacinto's faith remained steadfast through the child's illness but Magdala became more rebellious. Her inner antagonism was so acute she could no longer eat. She eventually wasted away to "skin and bones." Finally, Jacinto carried Magdala to the clinic to stay when she could no longer walk. Florence, seeing her dehydration, began to feed her intravenously. Somehow, inexplicably, the Lord began to work in Magdala's heart in a way she had not allowed before. Her whole attitude changed.

As the years passed, Jacinto became an elder in the church. He realized that God wanted him to serve in a distant part of the tribe. Florence asked Magdala, now with six small children, how she felt about moving. She answered, "I'm willing to go. Here I have a house and a little cornfield and the blessing of knowing God. I haven't suffered anything for my Lord, Who gave so much for me."

The entire family moved a three-day walk away from their past home to a new colony being cut out of the virgin forest where there was need for the help of a mature Christian worker. Jacinto supported his family by making tables and chairs out of the handsome red mahogany surrounding the village but his real work was with the people who needed to know Christ. The challenge was great for two tribes occupied the same village and cross-cultural clashes inevitably arose. Legal conflicts over the newly-appropriated lands caused deep-seated feuds.

Jacinto learned to give medicine and was able to keep many from needlessly dying from malaria and hookworm. His opportunity to witness for Christ enlarged far beyond his expectations when he had first agreed to leave his own home and fields and travel to a strange setting. He was, indeed, a missionary in his own right.

From the moment Florence opened the clinic door in the morning until she closed it at night, she was in a press of sick people. They rushed through their customary greetings to her so they could begin to enumerate their symptoms. The colorful terms in which they described their aches and pains had to be translated mentally into complaints she could diagnose; "the wind goes out" would be epilepsy, "white cough" would be tuberculosis, "stomach water" would be diarrhea.

Florence became very tired. Her energy disappeared. Her appetite lagged. Still she kept on. The need was too great for her to take the rest her body craved. Then one morning, she wakened completely jaundiced. That was the first time Florence admitted she could be seriously ill. We were heartbroken to see her leave us but she had to be flown home for complete rest.

She was in California for a few months with her parents, then anxious to get back to service again, she returned to Mexico too soon. By the time she reached Mexico City, she suffered a serious relapse of hepatitis and was laid up there another few months. We all missed her tremendously.

My family had been guardians and substitute parents to Mary Morison when she had first come to the States twelve years before. A bright butterfly of a girl, she had developed into a true Christian with a deep love for the Lord and for the Indians of Mexico. She had taken nurse's training and now was ready to undertake duties with Wycliffe. She came to Corralito to assist in Florence's absence and provided the light and laughter our grieved hearts needed. Mary was ready for anything!

Since she spoke Chol, a related language to Tzeltal, she soon picked up enough to keep on with the medical work. Her bright happy personality ministered when her human knowledge was limited. Nothing fazed her.

One time a contingent of fourteen soldiers on their way to another area stopped by for several days. Mary, accustomed to cooking for large groups on her father's coffee plantation, easily assumed this responsibility and was able to witness effectively of the Lord's graciousness while she was about it. Mary was with me at Corralito for the better part of a year. She was a delight to us all.

We learned more from the Indians about faith and trust than we were able to teach them. Unencumbered by sophisticated knowledge of "cause and effect" of germs, they prayed with utmost confidence for the Lord to heal what we knew were incurable diseases.

"Lord, you can do everything. You can heal this one," they would pray as they knelt around a patient beyond the help of medicine. We learned to do what we had never seen done in staid church circles at home. We knelt down on the ground at all hours of the day and night, sometimes many times a day, to pray for the sick. The Lord seemed to delight in answering these "impossible" requests. Patients with epilepsy were healed, others beyond human help were raised up, dying patients recovered. These first-generation Tzeltal Christians had the same kind of faith as first-century Christians in the days of the apostles.

Our faith was severely tested when fifteen-year-old Maria Kituk lay dying in childbirth. Her first baby had died and now after many agonizing days and nights, Maria lay on the bare planks of the family steambath, her face beaded with perspiration, unable to deliver her second child. Mary tried everything she knew to help Maria, without success. We stayed up with her until after midnight praying, hearing the young mother suffer, helpless as we watched her strength ebb. The baby was dead but still unborn. Maria was very near death.

At the pre-dawn prayer service in the *templo* Juan prayed, "Lord, we are like the Syro-Phoenician woman in the Gospel who would not take 'no' for an answer. You must save Maria's life!"

As Juan rose from his knees, he turned to us with a suggestion. Could we talk on the radio to our "brother," the pilot and ask him to fly someone to Corralito to save Maria's life? We raced home to communicate with MAF.

Within hours, the nurse from Jungle Camp, Marj Trulin, was on her way by plane. Marj was a gifted nurse with as much ability as many doctors and certainly more knowledge of assisting in primitive conditions. When her plane finally landed late that afternoon, we did not know if she had arrived in time. By the time she had walked from the airstrip to Maria's thatched-roofed hut, Mary had improvised an operating table and sterilized all the instruments. Numb with apprehension, the family looked on silently.

Maria's two older brothers who had adamantly refused to believe in the Lord, crouched in one corner of the hut. Outside in a cleared space beneath the orange trees, some believers gathered to pray for the one whose life hung in the balance and for those of us who were about to assist in the operation.

Maria herself was scarcely aware of what was happening as she was lifted gently to the table. A gasoline lantern was suspended from a rafter at a safe distance and the two nurses began to work over Maria to deliver the dead baby. Juan Mucha was entrusted to stand by her head with ether in one hand, counting so many drops per minute as he let the ether fall on a tea strainer held upside down over Maria's nose. A trained anesthetist could not have been gentler or more efficient than this Indian man participating in his first operation. Tomás Kituk, the young husband not yet out of his teens, stood tensely next to Juan, praying under his breath. Maria's mother-in-law stayed in the background, not daring to protest at the nurses' methods which differed so markedly from her primitive ones. My job was to explain to the family what the nurses were doing and to assist the nurses in whatever way they needed.

The Indians did not know it was my first operation as well as theirs!

During the hour and a half that Maria's life hung by a thread, we could hear the fervent pleas of thirty or more believers on their knees outside the hut. More than Maria's life was involved! If she lived, it would prove the believers' confidence in the Lord's power to answer prayer and would convince her unbelieving brothers who had refused to accept the Lord without signs and wonders.

Not until Maria was receiving fluid intravenously and had begun to show signs of returning to consciousness, did the nurses relax enough to report,

"Maria is going to live, thanks to God!"

To us who had known the slim possibilities for Maria's survival, it was a greater miracle than it appeared to be to the trusting Tzeltals who never for a moment questioned God's willingness to heal.

*Whosoever shall lose his life
for My sake
and the gospel's,
the same shall save it.*
Mark 8:35b

Florence was back!

Weakened and thinner,
she had finally recovered enough
to return to Corralito.

For days, believers trekked over the trails
to welcome her home.

They brought small gifts of eggs
and oranges and dried beans
but most of all,
they brought their love.

Chapter Fifteen

Martyrs

Florence marveled at how the babies had grown, greeted the children by name and inquired about the families at home. Life returned to "normal" or as normal as it would ever become at Corralito.

The group of three men, father and two teenage sons, stood apart from the others who were crowding Florence's small clinic. Their unadorned garb distinguished them as villagers from Tenango.

"Is there medicine here?" the older man asked.

Florence had never seen him at the clinic before, nor any other Tenango men for that matter. Tenango had been thoroughly hostile to the Gospel for all the years we had been ministering among the Tzeltals.

Glancing at the apparently healthy man and boys, Florence asked, "Who is sick?"

"My wife has been sick for many months," Sebastian explained. "We have carried her here because..." his voice faltered and he waved his right arm toward an inert form which lay on the ground some distance from the door.

Florence grasped the unfinished explanation. A man from Tenango would have tried every *shaman* in the area and spent every cent he had on liquor for them before he would have come for treatment at the Corralito clinic.

Years before, while we were still living at Yochib, a group of ten young men from Tenango had stopped by our house and had heard the Word of God. But when they returned to their own village with little red hymnals instead of candles and fire-rockets for a village *fiesta*, they had been beaten and the printed portions of the Word had been snatched from their hands and burned publicly. The irate village elders had shaken their black staffs in the faces of the boys and warned them against meddling with "another God." Thus, while the Spirit of God had been quickening other villages in the highland area, the village of Tenango had remained untouched.

It was a bleak spot, its high-peaked thatched huts huddling together on a windswept tableland halfway between high-country and low-country. The villagers had lacked the open friendliness some of the other Tzeltals exhibited even before the Gospel had come. We had made no impact on them, either with medicine or the Word.

Florence asked Sebastian and his two sons, erect Juan and deaf-mute Shep, to bring the ill lady into the clinic. With the lashings and blood-letting the *shamans* had imposed for a cure, she had grown steadily worse until she could no longer walk at all. Her responses to Florence's question-ings were barely audible. It did not take Florence long to perceive that her disease was incurable. It was one of those heartbreaking cases where a miracle would have been all that could possibly have saved her. But Florence did have medicine to ease the pain.

Sebastian and his sons dared not return to their own village while they were accepting assistance from us. One of the Christian widows invited them to share her flimsy hut of poles and grass thatch directly next to the chapel. The sick woman lay uncomplainingly on a straw mat on the hard-packed earthen floor. In the evening, with a cold damp wind blowing through the pole walls as if they did not exist, the family from Tenango shared the fire with the Corralito family. The widow and her two sons sang some of the hymns in Tzeltal. Then, before they pulled their thin cotton blankets over them for the night, they all would kneel together and ask the Lord to "work in the body and in the heart of the sick one."

With a son on either side of him, Sebastian began to attend Sunday services at the chapel. Gravely intent on every word of the message that the elders of Tenango had forbidden him to believe, Sebastian found his heart responding. From his sadly-depleted funds, he bought each of his sons a hymnbook, urging them to learn to read from the widow's sons so they could read God's Word for themselves when they returned to their own home. An older son, Cristóbal, came from Tenango with a load of corn to visit his dying mother. Sebastian urged him to hear "the good, new words" also. As the sick woman lay by the fire, listening to the singing of six hundred believers in the nearby chapel, she caught the meaning of the preaching and the prayers. Though God did not choose to heal her physically, He did heal the entire family spiritually.

One morning, Sebastian and his sons appeared at our door with the expected news. Instead of the usual pagan expression of hopelessness in the face of death, "it is ended," he used the new Christian terminology,

"My wife has gone to sleep in the Lord." Death had lost its sting.

A quandary presented itself to Sebastian in the next few weeks. It was a temptation to remain in Corralito where the believers were supportive and would help him "borrow" a plot of land for corn where he and his sons would be able to attend services regularly.

"But," he mused, "if I don't return to Tenango, who will tell the people of my village the Word of God?"

Cristóbal and his wife willingly welcomed Sebastian, Juan and Shep into their hut when they returned to Tenango. It was a time of enlightenment for them as they learned of the Lord from young Juan who read haltingly to them from the hymnbook.

Tenango seethed with hostility. When a few believers from Oxchuc visited to "strengthen their hands," a horde of aroused villagers encircled the house, forced their way into the hut and herded all the believers off to the village jail. For two days and nights, nine Oxchuc believers, plus five men and a boy from Tenango, were jammed into the tiny, filthy jail. For the first twenty-four hours, they had nothing to eat or drink.

Through the walls of their prison, they heard some of the townspeople plotting against them. They would burn some discarded "saint's" vestments, then accuse the believers before Oxchuc authorities of desecrating church property using the charred remains of the burned vestments as evidence.

Sunday morning, the town authorities let the prisoners out of jail. The believers from Oxchuc were ordered never to show their faces in Tenango again. Those from Tenango were publicly whipped in the town square but special wrath was reserved for Sebastian who had brought his "heretical" belief to the village. He was given fourteen lashes across his bare back with a hide whip.

Our service in Corralito was nearly over when the door of the *templo* was flung open and fourteen haggard men swarmed onto the platform. His homely face radiant with joy, Sebastian spoke for them all.

"The people of my village don't want God's Word to enter Tenango. They whipped us for believing in Him."

Baring his back, he displayed the glaring red welts inflicted by the lash.

"It didn't hurt," he said manfully. "All the time they beat me, I was thinking of the way Christ suffered for my sake."

One burly new believer had no stripes to show. "They whipped me, too," he explained a little defensively, "But it didn't leave a mark because I had my shirt on."

A greater price was yet to be paid.

Within months there were fifty believers from Tenango who met each Sunday to hear the Word of God. Sebastian was elected president of the new congregation.

Five days before the Christians in Tenango were to receive their first visit from the *mestizo* pastor and Indian elders, Sebastian made the half-day trip to Corralito. He wanted to borrow enough plates to feed all the expected visitors and he wanted to exchange news with the widow who had so kindly taken him into his hut when he had first arrived in Corralito.

"Yes, my sons and I are well. We have 'one heart' toward the Lord."

"No, I have not taken another wife. I have been too busy pastoring my flock of believers to look for one!"

"Did you know we plan to build a new chapel in Tenango soon on a hillside overlooking the whole village?"

"Yes, I'm glad we took God's Word to Tenango even though it's been hard for me and my sons. Even now, some of the villagers are blaming me because the rains are late. They claim it is my fault because I have believed in another God. They threaten to kill me but I am not afraid. I am ready to go be with the Lord."

Wednesday, August 10, 1955, was a day of triumph. By dawn, all of the Tenango believers had gathered at Sebastian's hut to prepare for the visit of the minister from Las Casas and the elders. Standing before the congregation to lead the singing, Sebastian felt a surge of joy. Two of the villagers who had been present when Sebastian had been taken off to jail had turned to the Lord. Some who had jeered when he was whipped publicly, now joined in the singing. Two town officials who had opposed the Gospel, had "entered in" themselves. God's Word had come to Tenango at last.

That night, after the visiting brethren had ridden on to the next chapel, Sebastian was summoned to pray for a sick person. Shep carried the victrola for his father. After playing the records for several hours and giving God's Word to the patient's family, Sebastian took a seat near the fire on a low wooden stool. He had just picked up an ear of corn when two shots at close range rang out.

Sebastian slumped forward. "It is for the Lord's sake that this has happened," he gasped. They were his last words.

It was not the last of God's work in Tenango. Government authorities stepped in to guarantee the right of anyone in the village to become an "*evangélico.*" One of the three murderers of Sebastian turned to the Lord. Others followed. Half of once-hostile Tenango eventually became Christian. A large new chapel stands today in Tenango, witness of a seed planted which gave forth new life abundantly.

The Word spread. Christian chapels sprang up in places distinctive for their picturesque names: Incense-Burner Spring, Deer Cliff, Meadow's Edge, Owl's House, Black Lord (named for the sacred mountaintop). In spite of threats, obstacles and hostility, twelve separate congregations of Indian Christians came into being within a day's radius of Corralito. Our chapel became the hub as God's work expanded in ever-widening circles throughout Tzeltal territory.

With the addition of each chapel, came a delegation of new believers requesting someone to preach God's Word to them. Not only was I responsible for preparing Tzeltal Scriptures but also I felt the urgency of preparing Tzeltal preachers.

Twice a week, preachers' classes met in our little hut. Joking good-naturedly with each other, the evangelists pulled up the wooden bench and crowded together on it. Mud-caked bare feet perched on a rung of the bench, they delved into their shirtfronts or net bags and pulled out printed portions of the Word they had come to study for that week's evangelization.

Teaching the Word provided a check on the translation I had worked on. Then, as these young men preached to their fellow-believers, another check was provided. If both the preachers and the listeners responded to the newly-translated Word in terms of a transformed life, the translation would have passed the most important test of all.

Before beginning the evening's study, my students bowed their heads to ask for help.

Our Lord, we don't know how to read well, we don't know how to preach well. But You have said in Your Book that You would help us to learn Your Holy Word. May Your Word "arrive" in our hearts, and in the hearts of all who hear it. May it not be in vain that we have it in our own language.

Their fellow preachers echoed "*Hichuk*" (Amen).

In the unaccustomed thrill of holding a book in their hands, Indians who had never heard of chapters and verses before, helped one another to find the place. As one of them read the passage we were to study, the others followed word for word in the printed portions propped open on their knees. Most of them were new readers who still stumbled over unfamiliar words, plowing past commas and periods without a pause. In a joint effort to reach the end of a passage without *me'tik*'s coming to the rescue, they prompted one another. From each tussle with the printed page, they emerged triumphant. They were reading words direct from God Himself!

Every head bent over their little books, intent on understanding what God said in His Word, they applied each word to their own hearts with a sense of wonder.

Don't let sin make servants out of your hands and feet for doing evil things,

they read in Romans. They stopped, convicted by the words.

"It is true, brothers. Our hands used to fight and kill. Our feet used to take us over the trail to steal, to drink and to attend *fiestas*." Their way of life stood condemned by the words on the page before them.

*But now, give yourselves to God. Let your hands
and feet serve Him,*

continued the rest of the verse.

They looked up from their books with as much
attentiveness as if God had spoken the words.

"Of course our hands and feet shall serve God.
We belong to Him."

Tears in my eyes, a thrill in my heart, I looked
at their unlovely, mud-caked feet propped on the
rungs of their benches and realized a new truth,

*How beautiful are the feet of them that carry good
tidings!*

The "preachers-of-the-Word" were not always
welcomed. Huts were barred to them. *Machetes*
were brandished in their faces. False accusations
were flung at them.

"You are tramping the trails because you are too
lazy to stay home and work!" There were cornfields to make and firewood to gather but the
Lord's work came before their own.

"You are deceivers, trying to get us to abandon
our patron saint in order to worship a god we can't
see!"

Thoughtfully they replied, "No, we are the ones
who have been deceived all these years into thinking wooden statues are alive. But now our eyes
have been opened by God's true Word."

"You are being paid by the *gringas* to spread
these lies!" was the most frequent claim.

"No, we don't expect pay on earth for spreading
God's Word. God will give us our pay in heaven,"
the believers countered.

Many times the preachers had to "*shake the
dust off their feet*" (to be more accurate, layers of

Chiapas mud) as witness that God's Word had been proffered and refused.

All along the way on their missionary travels, the evangelists gave out the Gospel.

"We did not want to be like the two men the Lord told about who came to someone in need on the trail and passed by on the other side. We stopped in every settlement to tell people about the Lord," they related triumphantly when they returned.

Some villagers in distant Lacandon asked for the message. There was no lack of volunteers to go although Lacandon was at least four days' journey away and it was made up of fugitives from justice! Killers were accustomed to making this tangled rain forest in the midst of hot country, a refuge from their pursuers.

Where sin abounded, grace was much more to abound.

From two missionaries temporarily assigned to Lacandon, we heard,

The visit of the Corralito believers has been the beginning of a work of the Spirit of God here! Everyone in the village except one couple gathered to hear God's Word preached by them and were profoundly moved. The day the Corralito believers left, the villagers spent the whole day learning hymns. On Sunday, they kept the Lord's Day for the first time with some of the young fellows preaching and praying publicly for the first time! The leader has burned his household fetish and they are making plans to build a chapel!

Lacandon became an all-Christian village. Once again, the Lord had prospered His Word.

"*Walk all over the world. Tell everyone the Good News,*" the Tzeltal version says. The Indian believers took these words literally. Tramping over the trails which crisscrossed the Oxchuc area with Gospel records in Tzeltal and eight Gospel Recording phonographs to help them explain "the good news", they stopped fellow-travelers on the trail, visited in hidden villages, entered isolated huts. Toughened, bare Tzeltal feet carried the Word into every crevice and fold of the Oxchuc hills. Hearts burning with the urgency of their mission, they let nothing deter them.

Answering an invitation to far-away Dry Mountain, crippled Martin Ensin with his Uncle Isidro found an entire family waiting to hear and believe. Isidro, remembering the account in the book of Acts about "Saul the persecutor" becoming "Paul the Apostle," was fired with the desire to propagate the faith he had once so violently opposed.

On their homeward journey, they had to pass through a *mestizo* town. Stopping to answer inquiries about the message they were spreading, they suddenly found themselves in the midst of wild turmoil. Church bells clanged angrily. Furious townspeople converged on them from all sides, flinging abusive words as well as rocks and sticks at them.

"Who sent you here to deceive with lies of the devil? We don't want heresy in our town! Never set foot here again!" shouted the maddened mob.

The defenseless evangelists were seized and propelled inside the town church. Their arms twisted agonizingly behind their backs, they were forced to kneel before the town's patron saint.

"But," Martin told us later, "even though they made our knees bow, they couldn't make our hearts bow to their gods of wood."

With blows raining on their bodies and a barrage of stones hurtling about their heads, Isidro and Martin were run out of town. Uncle Isidro, on his first evangelistic trip, was exultant. Just like the Apostle Paul, he, too, had been repaid with blows and curses for preaching the Gospel! He knew he was in good company.

The entrance of God's Word into Dry Mountain continued to give light. Two families gathered regularly to sing and pray until the ranchers and townspeople got wind of it. In the dead of night, nearly a hundred armed men from the town made their way over the uneven footpath leading to the isolated hut of the Santis brothers, the first believers in Dry Mountain. The crowd was determined to stamp out this belief.

While some of them surrounded the Santis' hut, others slashed up the thatched-roofed, plank-walled meeting-place with their long bush knives. They trussed up the two men believers and at rope's end, led them off to town. There a blood-thirsty mob had gathered at the summons of the church bells and threatened them with death. The two said calmly, "Go ahead and kill us. It will be for our faith in God and not for any crime we have done."

Disconcerted, the crowd fell back. They had lost their zest for bullying and buffeting. The believers were set free and God's Word took root in Dry Mountain.

Like a geographical listing of southern Mexico, towns were reached with the Gospel. Chanal, where believers were not even allowed to walk through the streets without being thrown into jail, went seven years before there was a single believer. Cancuc villagers, where intruders were murdered almost as a matter of routine, burned the homes of any who dared to profess a belief in Christ. And then, Bachajon, where we had been peremptorily refused entry after Bill's death, opened to the Word of God.

Located several mountain ranges beyond Oxchuc territory, Bachajon had symbolized Kipling's phrases:

Something lost behind the ranges...
Go and find it.

For many years we had lived within sight of those ranges, knowing that here lay one of the greatest challenges in all Tzeltal territory. Bachajon Tzeltal was the largest dialect of the entire language group.

No Oxchuc believer had ever set foot in Bachajon territory. The fourteen thousand Bachajon Tzeltals were noted for their pride, quick tempers and deadly *machetes*. Now the time had come.

Ten volunteers eagerly set off from Corralito one morning in a bone-chilling north wind. Their rubber raincapes shielded the victrola, the records and the printed portions of Tzeltal while the men themselves set off through ankle-deep mud, pants rolled up to their knees, disappearing into the clammy mist which blotted out the path before them. We knew they had embarked on the most difficult trip of their experience.

Two days' walk from familiar Oxchuc territory, these Indians from stony, sterile highlands penetrated deeper and deeper into the Bachajon forests, staring fascinated at the lush tropical growth which dwarfed them. Massive mahogany trees towered above, dropping pendulous vines from lofty treetops. Quick-moving lizards scurried over giant, fallen tree trunks to safety. Flocks of raucous parrots mounted up in sudden alarm, scolding the strangers for invading their haunts.

Through the vast, sparsely-inhabited pine forests they tramped for Bachajon huts were widely separated, often situated in nearly impregnable places so deep was their distrust of one another and of all outsiders. Nor were the preachers extended any welcome. At one hut after another, the Bachajon people peered suspiciously at them, refusing to give them lodging or to sell them food. They had to resort to gathering wild berries for sustenance. Water was equally hard to come by. One night, as they slept by the edge of the trail, a gentle rain fell and they were able to collect enough rain water in the folds of their raincapes to partially quench their thirst. They might have been able to shoot game for some of their needs but they had purposely left their guns at home, to avoid the suspicion of quarrelsome intent. Cacate'el, Cacwalha' were places Bill had visited many long years ago and where Florence and I had attempted to gain a toehold six years before. This group visited these towns. Some they met on the trail did not want to hear the Word of God.

"Go back where you came from," they were told at gunpoint. Still they persisted until they came to the very edge of Bachajon territory by the bank of the swift-running Paxilha' River.

Wherever they were allowed, the beginning evangelists played the Gospel records, explained the Word of God or left a portion of the written message.

They had started back toward the mountain range, hazy in the distance, when they were overtaken by a lithe, well-built Bachajon man. His wide-brimmed hat, set at a jaunty angle with an iridescent *quetzal* feather twisted around the crown as a hatband, topped an intelligent face. His hazel eyes searched theirs before he asked,

"Are you the ones who have brought God's Word?"

"Yes," the Corralito believers replied readily. "Do you want to hear about the living God?"

"I have already heard God's Word," he offered. Surprised, the men sat beside the trail while Santiago Gomez told his story.

Six years before, he and five others had met Florence and me when we had spent a month trying to contact some of the Bachajon Tzeltals. Intrigued by the victrola and records which spoke Tzeltal, he had bought the victrola and taken it home with him. He had played the records repeatedly for his family and others to hear but had had no other contact with Christians until he caught up to the Corralito believers on the trail. When he learned we were now located at Corralito, he promptly decided that he would accompany the men back so he could learn more.

Heavy footsteps interrupted the translation of Hebrews I was working on. I had not known when to expect the young preachers back from their missionary journey nor did I recognize the lean, alert young man in *mestizo* clothes with a green-gold *quetzal* feather entwined around his hat. The feather betrayed his origin; he was from the Bachajon forests! When he introduced himself, I remembered quick-speaking Santiago Gomez with his eager questions and insistence on owning his own victrola with records.

"I remember! Six of you came from a far-off place called Paxilha' and said you wanted to believe. I took a picture of all six of you listening to the records. Are the others believers, too?"

Santiago shrugged his shoulders sadly. "Four of them have died. Two of them were my own younger brothers."

In the Bachajon forests where the only remedy for sickness is witchcraft, death often comes early and suddenly.

"But my older brother Manuel and I have believed God's Word and have told many others."

God in His faithfulness had not allowed His Word to return to Him without fruit.

Santiago stayed with us a week at Corralito. With his help, we were able to record a number of Bible readings with explanations in his Bachajon dialect. While we sent the tape off to be pressed in Mexico City into two full records, we sent him back to Paxilha' with one thousand copies of a hymnal we had run off on our little mimeograph.

Santiago returned to Paxilha' with a strong witness. Within a few months, a healthy nucleus of believers had begun to gather regularly for singing and prayer and discussion of the little they knew of God's Word. It was new and fresh to them and they fed on it as hungry children. Juan Moreno was a particularly promising new believer.

One day, he appeared, breathless, in Santiago's doorway.

"I came to see if you are all right," he said to Santiago. "Some say that men are coming to kill you."

Instead of going out to his cornfield that day where he would have provided an open target for his enemies, Santiago gathered his family about the little victrola and played the records to reassure them all. By mid-morning, Juan Moreno stood up to stretch his legs and walked over to the open doorway. A volley of shots rang out, hitting him in the chest. He toppled over without a word and lay dead in the doorway. Santiago saw the sunlight glinting on the rifle barrels of men halfhidden in the bush. He realized he had been the target of their bullets, not Juan Moreno. Racing across the open stretch of clearing toward the forest wall behind his house, he plunged into the shelter of thick vines and underbrush. Bullets whined about his head but none struck him. He did not find his wife and children until the next day.

They had attempted to follow Santiago but, with bullets nicking Jeronima in four different places, she had sunk down in complete terror at the base of a huge tree. There she had spent the night with the children huddled against her.

The killers, thinking they had struck down Santiago, rushed up to hack Juan Moreno's inert body to pieces. Infuriated that their prey had escaped, they set fire to the Gomez hut. Every possession in the world this little family had acquired, went up in smoke. From a rise in the forest, Santiago watched it burn.

Somehow, the other Christians in Paxilha' discovered his whereabouts and followed him, fearful of the same treatment. For a week, they slashed their way through dense tropical jungle with their *machetes*, following a swift-flowing river which cut through the tangled rain forest like a knife gash. When they hoped to take refuge at a ranch, they were driven off like dogs. No one offered them food or shelter. They learned to avoid every sign of human habitation. By day, they eased their hunger by roasting the few ears of dried corn they had brought with them. By night, they slept fitfully along the trail making improvised brush shelters to keep off the heavy dew.

When they finally reached a safe place, the compound of an American missionary in Chol territory, they were weak from exposure.

Eventually, the bedraggled group found its way to Corralito. Here the Christians bathed them in sympathy, bringing little gifts of food to them from their own sparse supplies.

"Poor things! It is for God's sake that they have lost everything they own!"

Then to further reassure them, they went on to add, "Don't let your hearts be sad. God will make your hearts big. God will replace all you have lost. God will work in your village."

We knew it would be true in Bachajon. In the highland village of Tenango where humble Sebastian had given his life nine months before, a fervent group of Christians now existed.

Except a corn of wheat
fall into the ground and die,
it abideth alone.
But if it die, it bringeth forth much fruit.

A government investigation, instigated by a well-educated Bachajon schoolteacher, brought some justice to Santiago. The inciter of the evil plot was Estéban, a saloonkeeper on Bachajon's one cobblestone street. One afternoon at the height of the *fiesta* of San Miguel, he had plotted openly to do away with the "sect" Santiago had brought from Corralito. Estéban was haled into court, jailed for three days and fined twelve thousand *pesos*. The Christians began to meet in Paxilha' again and to spread their faith.

It was not the end of the story of Bachajon - only the beginning.

The hand of the Lord
shall be known toward His servants...
Isaiah 66:14b

Florence laid a gentle, quieting hand
on Maria Kituk's shoulder.

The young woman was gasping
in great long sobs,
as much from fear as from actual pain.

She had good cause to fear -
her first three babies had been born dead
after many long days of difficult labor.

Now, this fourth little one was coming early.

Chapter Sixteen

Clinic

Florence had scheduled an operation for Maria in Tuxtla at the end of June to see if, for once, Maria could deliver a healthy child. But the Kituks had waited too long to tell her Maria had gone into early labor. Now, it was too late. Still, she had to try.

I dashed to the radio transmitter to see if I could raise the MAF base in Ixtapa. It was past time for our regularly-scheduled call but they answered anyway. Within minutes, the pilot was on his way in a little Piper plane to pick up Florence and Maria.

While those of us at Corralito gathered to pray, Tomás tied his frightened wife into a straight chair. Then, suspending it by a leather strap across his forehead, he set out up the steep rocky trail to the airstrip, a half hour away.

"Kill me, kill me, I'm going to die!" Maria screamed. In the plane, she half-sat, half-lay in the rear seat while Florence sat beside the pilot, turning uncomfortably to keep an eye and a comforting hand on her terrified patient. The plane hit an air pocket and dropped in a rush. Maria's cries suddenly ceased. Quietly, she said to Florence,

"*Me'tik, talix te alale*" (The baby has come).

Twisting herself around enough to see, Florence observed two bluish legs and feet.

Within five minutes, the pilot had landed and pulled to a stop in front of the hangar at Ixtapa.

There were no medical facilities available there but at least Maria could be laid out on a straw mat for a more comfortable delivery.

The baby had still not been fully born. Florence, noting the deep grayish coloring, was certain it was dead. Acutely aware of poor Maria's past history and of her own inexperience as a midwife, she knelt in front of her patient and prayed aloud in Tzeltal with unaccustomed facility. With no time for a proper scrub, one of the MAF wives poured alcohol over Florence's trembling hands. Maria's contractions had stopped and she apparently had no more strength to help with the delivery.

Slipping her right hand under the back and head of the baby, Florence slowly maneuvered it out. The little body was limp, dark as death and unmoving. Someone discovered a small infant's syringe in a medicine cabinet, swished alcohol through it and Florence suctioned out mucus from the baby's nose and throat. The tiny girl could not possibly live. Then, after long, long moments, she suddenly gasped once. Another gasp and she was breathing and crying! Never had they heard a more beautiful sound! For a whole hour the infant cried, turning from pale pink to bright red.

Like all Tzeltal women, accustomed to losing many infants at birth, Maria Kituk had no clothes for the baby. A couple of old, washed rags, a stringy hair ribbon to bind the baby's arms close to its body,and a faded, worn skirt of her own were all Maria had for covering for this most precious gift of God. The MAF wives generously supplied warm clothing and blankets for the dainty baby girl. The premature birth had doubtless saved the baby's life for Maria could not safely deliver a full-sized infant.

Two years later, Maria and Tomás became parents of a son born by Caesarian section in Tuxtla. Whenever we visited them, they would say,

"We thank you and God for these children. They are yours and His."

Ever aware of the spiritual needs of the Tzeltal Indians, we realized that we could never begin to meet their physical needs with the inadequate facilities we had at Corralito. So immediate were these desperate conditions, it seemed almost hopeless to deal with the soul until the body could at least be made comfortable enough to heed.

Avis Crowder, R.N., was the Lord's catalyst at this point. She and Florence had both accepted the Lord during their medical training at Mt. Zion Hospital in San Francisco. They had come as partners to Mexico City at the urging of Dawson Trotman, head of the Navigators. But Avis had been forced to return to California when she developed incipient tuberculosis and Florence had then joined me at Yochib. Now years later, Avis was well enough to come join us when we most needed her. Her training in dentistry and laboratory techniques was invaluable.

Soft-spoken Avis entered wholeheartedly into the work with no need for transitional adjustment. She loved the Indians. They loved her. In a letter to my parents soon after she arrived in Corralito, she described the vision the Lord had given her:

Just at dusk we went into the chapel to begin the service and as we were singing in the near-darkness, the thought occurred to me again, "What should my prayer for these people be?" I seemed to hear the Lord's words, "Ask, and it shall be done."

I looked out into the audience into the face of old Marcos, the chief, whose salvation is in itself a mighty miracle and thought of the utter devotion with which he now serves Christ.

Again I seemed to hear the Lord asking, "Is anything too hard for me?"

Why should I not ask for the salvation of the whole tribe? But such a request would be so fantastic! Then I decided that in view of the fact that the one to whom my prayer was addressed was the Creator of heaven and earth with power beyond the ability of man to fathom and, since His own desire for man's salvation is such that He sent His Son to purchase man's redemption, I must ask that the time might come when there would not be a Tzeltal of accountable age living on the earth who was not a redeemed soul. And even as I thought of the magnitude of the task of seeking out, evangelizing and winning every single Tzeltal to Christ, the Lord seemed to say to me, "The zeal of the Lord of hosts will perform this. The power belongs to Me. Man is expected only to believe and obey".

Then the sweetest peace settled over me. I thought of the crosses I had seen that day by the water holes, of the caves we had passed where Satan is still worshipped, of the houses we passed where Marianna had said, "An unbeliever lives there." And the Lord flooded my heart with the assurance that the time would come when none of these things would any longer exist in this land but instead in every hut would be His children and chapels and temples would grace the land from border to border.

Avis, a visionary at heart, began to dream. With almost no funds to work with, she drew up plans for a new, spacious clinic, the like of which had never been seen in Indian country. We presented the project to the Tzeltal leaders. In turn, they enlisted the labor of all the Indian believers in every chapel throughout the region.

"We don't have anything else to give the Lord, but we can give our time and strength," they all agreed with enthusiasm.

On a steep hillside overlooking a patchwork of cornfields, the House of Medicine began to take shape. Its site had to be leveled from a precipitous hill by men whose only tools were a few spades and a crowbar. Because timber was scarce in that altitude, the laborers felled trees many miles distant then conveyed them by brute force up and down hills and across streams. Immense rocks were dragged, carried or rolled to make up the foundation for the clinic was to be two stories high! Jugful by jugful, the women and children brought up the necessary water for making thousands of bricks which were then molded, dried in the sun and stored until needed. During the day, the Indian brothers joked and labored together. At noon, they squatted on the ground to eat their coarse, soured, unheated food brought from home. At the end of the day's work those who lived too far away to go home each night, sang cheerfully and prayed together before stretching out wherever they happened to be, to get some sleep. Chapel by chapel they worked, a week at a time. The only paid workmen were a *mestizo* Christian mason and his son who worked side by side with the Tzeltals instructing them in the necessary rudiments of a sturdy foundation. The Reformed Mission in Chiapas made a grant of $2,000.

The town president ordered the Christians to work on the town hall instead of on the clinic. He refused to grant a deed to the land on which we were building. When it was time to burn lime for the whitewashing of the walls, the men could not find enough limestone.

Discouragements only served to propel them forward. When an obstacle appeared insurmountable, the believers prayed. Within six months, a substantial two-story clinic of eleven rooms with windows, hinged doors, a dental area, a long waiting room, a ward with beds for the more seriously ill patients and even an embryo laboratory with microscope and slides, testified of the Lord's interest in His Tzeltal children.

As she moved her supplies from the old mud hut with crumbling walls and bare dirt floor, Florence marveled,

What a pleasure! Turn on a faucet and there's water! No need to send to the river with a clay jug. Sweep the tile floor - no facefuls of dirt. New shipment of medicine - adequate storage space. An acutely ill patient and we can place him on a wooden bed in the patients' room instead of trying to care for him while he lies outside on the ground.

A wide deep porch fronted the outside of the clinic where patients waited their turn out of the sun and rain. Upstairs were three large rooms for living quarters. The spaciousness and conveniences of the new building were a thrill to us all. But to the Tzeltals, it meant more than that - it meant HOPE!

From many trails high in the hills, this glistening white clinic with its aluminum roof spelled a haven from the fear of witchcraft as well as relief from illness. One old deacon from the congregation stated, "I want to be carried here when I am dying. It is such a nice place to die."

The critically ill patients were kept clean and comfortable in the patients' room with their families close by to provide food and care for them. It was not only medical care which they received at the clinic, though. There was the encouragement of fellowbelievers, prayer during the day as emergencies arose, singing, Bible-reading and prayer each evening. In fact, there was an occasional patient who had to be persuaded he was well enough to leave the clinic so much did he enjoy the fellowship there!

The clinic became a magnet of hope to Indians from all over the tribe. Unbelievers as well as believers began to discover that medicine and prayer were more effective than the old-fashioned pulse-taking of the *shamans*. Florence and Avis often treated more than a hundred patients a day.

They could not do it alone. Dedicated Tzeltal Christians began to help in the work. With basic training, they learned to assist in some of the routine medical work. Our first helper was Domingo Mucha who had been a former herb doctor. His natural aptitude for medical work enabled Domingo to learn quickly how to give skillful injections and suture wounds. His firsthand experience as an herb doctor provided him with the opportunity to point out the difference between trusting in the Lord and using rites of magic! He loved to use the microscope. His keen eyes, once so proficient at spotting animal tracks, now became expert at spotting microscopic parasites: hookworm, roundworm, whipworm, pinworm, tapeworm, amoeba. And when an occasional patient indicated some reluctance to take the medicine prescribed, Domingo was wise enough to let him peer through the microscope and see what caused his miseries!

Another Tzeltal who became a clinic helper was Tomás Kituk. He had originally come to the clinic to get help in arithmetic for he served as church treasurer and needed assistance in adding up the church offerings accurately. Tomás did not need to be convinced of the value of medical care - his wife and two children owed their lives to it. However, he was not particularly apt in the beginning. Eventually he learned to file and to locate any of the hundreds of patients' charts. Then with furrowed brow, Tomás set about mastering the microscope. The harder the task, the harder he prayed. Tomás literally "prayed his way" into becoming a valuable clinic assistant.

He was especially fascinated with the art of pulling teeth. Florence taught him where to inject novocaine and how to hold the dental forceps. When the day arrived for his third lesson, Florence was too ill to leave her bed. She urged Tomás to care for the waiting dental patients. With beads of sweat dotting his brow, Tomás pulled his first tooth. Another patient waited with swollen jaw and anguished expression. Tomás took off his shirt and with sweat and prayer, pulled his second tooth. Even though their "dentist" was a raw amateur, his patients were grateful, for a painless extraction was preferable to the old way of jabbing a heated nail into an aching tooth.

And still we needed more help. Since the men were busy with their cornfields and their wives with the keeping of the family, Florence tried to train some of the unmarried girls. Usually, parents did not allow their young daughters out of their sight and it took some persuading on Florence's part to bring a few girls from their homes into the clinic for medical training. There were many ways in which these girls could be useful such as washing bottles, mopping floors, packaging each dose of medicine singly, cleaning wounds and folding bandages. We needed women to treat ill women. Finally, after much deliberation, the parents of five girls consented to allow them to come for training.

It was not a good idea. One of the girls was willing to perform "important" tasks such as giving injections but she did not want to do "menial" tasks such as cleaning up afterwards. Another enjoyed gazing at the bustling activity meanwhile blocking sinks and doorways through which the harried nurses were trying to move rapidly. Unaccustomed to positions as "*me'tik*'s helpers," some of the girls abused their privileges by giggling or by speaking to men not in their own clan or by dawdling on the trail home. There was talk.

Again, God gave the answer. Two young wives without children wanted to serve the Lord. Both were mature enough to do what they were asked to do and they insisted on doing it without pay. The Lord rewarded these young women for one was able to adopt two infants and the other had one of her own.

The town president never gave up in his opposition to the clinic. One time, he manipulated the other officials into demanding that Tomás Kituk give up his work in the clinic in order to take a political position in Oxchuc. For weeks, the decision hung in the balance. Finally, God's intervention was clear. The very ones who had made the demand reversed themselves and said, "We will not force the ones at the clinic to serve here in town. They are serving in other ways."

Months later, when a survey team needed the underbrush cleared for boundary lines through Oxchuc, the town president again ordered the clinic to be closed so all the workers could get to work with their *machetes*. Protests did no good.

Then, a few days before our medical helpers were to report for duty, the righthand man of the *mestizo* engineer was carried to our clinic, near death from dysentery. Domingo and Tomás administered intravenous fluids with other medications and he recovered.

When the engineer, himself, visited the clinic to check on the progress of his assistant, he could not contain his surprise at the improvement.

"What did you do for him?" he asked the two medical assistants. They told him.

"Fine," he said. "Keep on with your medical work."

Domingo shook his head. "We won't be able to," he explained. "We have been ordered to close the clinic to work for you."

The engineer was indignant. "I'm the one who gives the orders, not the town officials. You remain here at your job in the clinic."

Our medical work continued to flourish. Not only were Domingo and Tomás learning but evangelists were going out to serve elsewhere and leaders from far-off chapels saw the need to set up small dispensaries to alleviate the suffering of their own people. Florence taught them as best she could at Corralito with on-the-job instruction and then with classes after hours. And still it was not enough.

She developed a handbook for her medical personnel. She wrote,

How wide-eyed and open-mouthed they were as we taught them about the wonders of the human body, the properties of microbes, the life cycle of intestinal parasites, the functions of vitamins and minerals and of hitherto unimagined things such as grams, cubic centimeters and percentages! And

how taxed we were to express some of these concepts in their Indian language!

But translate them she did. With the assistance of Beverly Ernst, another nurse with special training in microbiology who helped us for more than a year, Florence wrote a series of handbooks in Tzeltal on diagnosis and treatment, a manual of laboratory techniques and another about the extraction of teeth. The thirty-five medical workers she trained could refer to the printed page in their own language. She also prepared an illustrated hygiene chart simple enough for even the illiterate to grasp.

To combat the idea of witchcraft being the cause of illness, she headed the chart, "What Causes Illness," and depicted all sorts of tiny microbes as seen through a microscope.

On the left column of the chart were the words, "Things It Is Not Good to Do." On the right column were the words, "Things It Is Good to Do." These were accompanied by attractive drawings depicting the actions described.

Don't allow chickens and dogs
to wander in and out of your hut at will.Don't get
your drinking water
from waterholes where pigs wallow.
Don't drink from the same gourd
as a sick person.
Do boil your drinking water.
Do wear sandals to keep from getting hookworm.
Do wash your hands thoroughly
before handling food.

At the bottom of the chart was the reminder
from Scripture:

Your bodies are the temple of the Holy Spirit.

Along with the literacy program came little
booklets of hygiene thus serving a dual purpose -
training the beginning readers to take care of their
health as well!

There was also the huge responsibility to choose
medical trainees with great care and prayer.
Knowing how much training is required in our
society, it sometimes seemed presumptuous to in-
struct people as uneducated as these Tzeltals in
the art of giving medicine. Would lives be en-
dangered or helped? Would God really be honored
through it? After much deliberation, we decided
He wanted us to work toward the abolishment of
physical ignorance as much as spiritual ignorance.

One after another, the new "medicine-givers"
opened dispensaries in strategic spots throughout
the highland area. Chief Marcos Ensin's son,
Martin, in spite of his congenitally deformed
hands, capably cared for the sick in the new clinic
the Pakwina believers built. Workers from Tenango, Cancuc and other distant settlements supple-
mented their evangelistic message with medical
healing. With gifts from American Christians,
Florence was able to equip each of her medical
workers with thermometers, hypodermic syringes,
a pressure cooker for sterilizing the instruments
and a kerosene stove. Christian "medicine-givers"
replaced the tribal *shamans* and provided hope
where there had been none.

Heaven and earth shall pass away,
but My words shall not pass away.
                                    Matthew 24:35

It's coming, *me'tik!* It's coming!"

The child's hearing was keener than mine
for I heard nothing
but the sounds of the crowd milling about.

Our tiny airfield was alive
with excited Tzeltals
that Saturday early in August of 1956.

Chapter Seventeen

The Call

Children called to each other in their high-pitched little voices. Their parents, dressed in their finest garments with extravagant red and orange embroidery, were only slightly more calm. Dogs dashed between the forest of human legs, yapping as if they, too, shared in the festivities.

Then we heard it! The drone of the small yellow plane belonging to MAF gradually grew louder. It was bearing the most precious cargo the Indians had ever hoped for - the New Testament in Tzeltal. God at last was speaking to them in their own language! The blue sky was washed clear of the clouds which had filled it for days on end. The little plane circled then slipped among the jagged, jade-colored peaks about the airstrip, took a sharp right turn and was on the ground! No matter that it bounced a little over the rough runway, it came to a quick stop and the door was flung open.

"Here it is," called Hatch with a wide grin. He held up a package in a triumphant gesture. It was immediately grasped by an eager Indian hand, then other hands stretched to reach for Hatch's treasured shipment. Before anyone could alight, the packages were handed down, to be handled with awe, even unopened.

Florence and I could not wait. Like children at Christmas, we snatched one package and unceremoniously undid the string. In the middle of the airstrip with every eye upon us, we lifted out the first copy of the Oxchuc New Testament.

Crowding close to see the first book in their language, the Tzeltals stood hushed in momentary wonder. Then there was a babble of exclamations.

Ach' Testamento in gold letters on a handsome cover of simulated brown leather. The size.... The weight.... The thickness.... Never had there been such a book!

I caught Florence's eyes. They were filled with tears. All the years of labor, of patience, of frustration, of disappointment, of hope deferred - all were culminated in this printed Word! A tremendous force had been released among the highland Tzeltals.

There was no lack of volunteers to carry the precious packages the twenty minutes it took to go over the trail to the clinic. Grinning men delightedly balanced cartons of New Testaments on their shoulders. Little boys struggled manfully with boxes too heavy for them, finally letting their elders take over. I carried that first copy over the trail myself, too touched to let it out of my hands.

Hatch made many trips that day to bring us the rest of the New Testaments and the distinguished guests for the jubilant dedication the next day.

From hamlet to village, from every tiny settlement throughout the Oxchuc region, came expectant Indians that Sunday. Some brought tight bunches of red-orange sand orchids to hang from the *templo* rafters. Others spread pungent pine needles over the hard-packed dirt floor. Six hundred tightly-packed worshippers filled the benches, overflowing into the aisles. Another six hundred crowded the open windows and doors, eager to see within. The Indian deacons had opened all the boxes of New Testaments and stacked them as they did their corn, in neat, precise rows by the edge of the platform. Behind the impressive pile of books sat the Indian elders in spotless handwoven native garments with red sashes, their customarily unruly hair neatly combed. In the presence of so many distinguished visitors, they made a valiant effort to repress their high spirits.

Daniel Aguilar, the minister representing the Spanish-speaking churches, rose to speak. With his customary poise, he addressed his Indian brothers in a firm voice.

Brethren in Christ, do you receive, believe, and promise to proclaim to others the Word of God that will be put in your hands today?

As in one voice, the thronged church chorused a determined, *"Yak!"* (yes).

From our vantage point behind the portable organ, where Florence and I shared a wooden bench, we singled out one after another in the hushed audience, recalling how God had already used His Word in their lives.

Nick Nich, his close-cropped grey head standing out above others in the crowd, had put away his second wife when he heard that God had given Adam only one wife.

Heavy-set Sebastian Mucha, scarred veteran of many drunken brawls, had never taken another drink after hearing that God disapproved of drunkenness.

Affable Lorenzo Yuba, whom the tribal leaders had chosen to be the *capitán* of the next *fiesta*, had ceased his participation when he believed on the Lord.

And over on the women's side next to each other, sat wives number two and number three of gruff old *shaman*, Alonzo Pe. They had heard the

Word of God one Sunday in church and adamantly refused to follow the irate old man home again. The Word of God had already wrought a deep change in many hearts. In printed form, it would work in the hearts of many more.

Señor Francisco Estrello, representative of the American Bible Society, read from the Tzeltal translation of Paul's epistle to the Thessalonians:

When the good new words reached you, they had an impact on your hearts, because of the power of God, and because of the Holy Spirit.

The first-generation Tzeltals were like the first-century Thessalonians!

You considered God's Word great. You suffered for it. Your hearts rejoiced over it.

Paul might have been writing to the Oxchuc Tzeltals rather than to the Thessalonians!

You left false gods. You turned your hearts around toward God. You gave yourselves to serve the real living God, and you are waiting for His Son Jesus to come from heaven....

The words could have been written about the hundreds of Tzeltal Christians gathered together to thank God that His Book had come to them.

From the top of the pile of New Testaments, Señor Estrello took three copies. One he handed to me, one to Juan Mucha and one to Domingo Mucha. The two who had helped to translate every word of it for their people would be the first two to possess a copy. Eyes alight with joy, they grasped their copies of God's Book as if they intended never to let them out of their hands.

"Now I won't lose any of God's words out of my heart," Juan exulted, "because they are all written down on paper."

More enduring than the intricate hieroglyphs of their Mayan forebears carved on stone stelae were the printed words of their New Testament which spelled out a new way of life for the Tzeltals.

Wide bars of sunlight, slanting through the high windows above the platform, converged on the pulpit as if it were a sundial. It was mid-afternoon and the service was drawing to a close. Some in the congregation had stood the whole time, grateful to have a spot from which they could see and hear. Even the babies had refrained from crying as lustily as they sometimes did. No one had thought of the passage of time. It had been a momentous day, the day God's Book arrived.

Juan Mucha stood up to lead the closing prayer. With a love-filled voice, as if only he and the Lord were present, Juan prayed out of the fulness of his own heart,

Lord, thank You for giving us Your Book. But may we not only have Your Word in our language. May we also have it written in our hearts.

The sun was exploding in a final burst of glory against the highest mountain peaks when I finally started homeward alone from the *templo*. In the crook of my arm, I carried my own cherished copy of the Oxchuc New Testament. Strangely, I did not feel elated. My mission in Oxchuc was accomplished. Yet, there were many others who still needed to hear.

There were the spirited Tenejapa Tzeltals with their sacred crosses at every waterhole.

And the uninhibited Cancuc Tzeltals still worshipped a Black Christ in their wild mountain villages.

Too, there were the seldom-contacted Bachajon Tzeltals where we had tried to enter years before.

I shelved my thoughts. There was too much to be done here.

The New Testament had arrived in Corralito at a most strategic time. The self-contained world of Oxchuc had previously consisted of the cornfields belonging to one's clan, the footpaths leading to the huts of kin and the many annual *fiestas* commemorating one or another religious festival. Now alien ideas from beyond their borders permeated the isolated villages. Footpaths had turned into well-traveled horse trails. Schools were springing up in each settlement and children of illiterate adults were learning to read. Well-groomed outsiders appeared more often in the region. Some of them warned the Indians against the two *gringas* who were "advance agents of a greedy country called the United States which threatened to take away Oxchuc's only asset, the stony soil on which grew only one crop, corn."

Others warned them against the dangerous doctrine the two *gringas* were spreading. What confusion to untutored Indians whose horizon had been bound by the vertical crags that hemmed them into the hollows where they had been born! An insidious influence threatened to blight the witness of the Tzeltal church. One of our most promising schoolteachers, a former preacher-in-training, defected. Some of the weaker believers went back to drinking and brawling. Like the blight which often attacked the most carefully-planted cornstalks, turning them yellow and useless from the root up, the backsliding began to spread.

Florence and I were dismayed. Just at the time when everything should have been greatly progressing, we seemed to be facing serious regression. What was the answer? We could not allow the forces of Satan to snatch back those who had so recently left him! We fell on our knees and cried to the Lord for His answer. We had done our best, and it was not enough. When it came, His answer was very clear.

The only defense against such devastating blight was the Word of God. A thorough grounding in scriptural principles was an absolute necessity. It was not enough to give the Indians the Word; we had to instill it in them so firmly that they could not forget what it meant.

Be ye doers of the Word, and not hearers only.

James 1:22 became a vital admonition to them.

We sent word to all the far-flung congregations - a Bible School for concentrated study of the New Testament they had just received would be held in Corralito from December 3 through 14. God's Word had brought the Tzeltal church into being; God's Word would make it invincible.

The practical need to feed one hundred fifty men for two weeks, three times each day, was a challenge. Rains had been scanty and late that year and food was scarce. Humble volunteers traveled many miles over the trails to bring food as their "gift to God." Women brought their cooking pots and water jugs. We had more than we needed.

The week the Bible School was to begin, torrential rains descended to turn the trails into miry ruts. The weather deterred no one. From far-off Lacandon had come several lean young men, long forelocks of hair secured behind their ears, sent by their villagers to learn more of God's Word and bring it back to them. Pakwina, Yochib, Oxchuc, Tenango, Cancuc - from wherever the Gospel had

taken root, eager representatives had gathered for
the most intensive Bible Study any of them had
undertaken.

Paul Meyerink of the Reformed Church of
America had been assigned to the Tzeltals just
seven months before. He taught a course called
"Introduction to the New Testament" while I interpreted for him. In the late morning, I taught the
Book of Romans, a study rich and valuable for the
Tzeltals who were to return with these great truths
to their own people. Later in the afternoon, I
taught a course in Church History to acquaint our
preachers with some of the great heroes of the faith
and to impress upon them the fact that they
formed part of a worldwide community called, "The
Christian Church."

No seminary professor ever faced more attentive students than I did every morning. Faces still
damp from water splashed on them from the icy
stream, they swarmed into the low-roofed chapel
some of them still drying their hands on their hair.
Over a hundred earnest young men from twenty
different congregations filled the benches, open
New Testaments on their knobby knees, leafing
through to find the portion of the Word they were
to study that day. Some new readers puzzled over
chapter and verse until a companion pointed it out
to them. Deacons from Corralito slipped in to listen when they were finished with their meal
chores.

As vibrant as the day the words were written,
Paul's message struck answering hearts,

*I have a debt...to tell the good new words to those
who have never heard.*

Some sucked in their breath on one side of their
mouths to indicate they were convicted of owing a

debt, also. They now had the entire New Testament in their own hands while less fortunate members of the tribe had never heard God's Word.

Chapter by chapter, the Indian students went through the book of Romans with me.

"God knows all about us, doesn't He?" they remarked with shame after reading the list of sins in chapter one. These verses had not been difficult to translate; Tzeltal had a plethora of words for sin!

But chapter three had not been so easy for terms like *"grace," "righteousness," "propitiation"* and *"justification"* had no ready-made counterparts in Tzeltal.

God's heart is straight and He makes straight the heart of those who believe/obey Jesus.

They understood. "Straight-heartedness" became a new word in Tzeltal and it took the place of more sophisticated words.

We who have died to sin, as it were, should not go on sinning.

Though some of the young preachers might have been tempted to deal lightly with sin, they realized that God did not consider it lightly.

Sober, intense, newly-converted Domingo Mendez from Bachajon stood up, gripping the back of the bench in front of him.

Brethren, my hands and feet used to serve sin, just as God says. My fists found anyone who laid a hand on me. My feet took me off to find liquor at all hours of the day and night. But from now on my hands and my feet are going to serve God.

Domingo Mendez returned to the Bachajon forests to become as powerful a leader for good as he had once been for evil among his own people.

The final day of the Bible Institute arrived. Our Indian preachers felt a great reluctance to leave the fellowship of other Christians. Back in their isolated clearings throughout the hills, they would remember the times of singing, praying and testifying, and it would steady them for the hostility some of their kinsmen would display.

Bowing their shaggy black heads in humility over their New Testaments, they thanked the Lord, breaking down in tears as they recalled the precious lessons learned.

Lord, we have a debt to tell others about You. Help us to pay our debt like the Apostle Paul paid his, by taking Your Word everywhere...

• Personable, outspoken Elder Feliciano Pe rose quickly to his feet. "I will go to Lacandon," he offered. The four believers from Lacandon who had been begging for someone to teach them more about the Lord could not contain their joy!

• Slight, soft-spoken Deacon Tomás Ch'ijk also volunteered to leave his hut and cornfield to take the Word over the intervening mountain ranges to Bachajon.

• Tall, young Juan Mena with his broken nose and infectious grin, spoke up, stating he was willing to go to the border of Cancuc territory to start an evangelical school and act as shepherd to a group of new believers there.

• Juan Ch'ijk, a new elder, asked to be sent to fanatical Tenango, though it might mean the risk of his life.

The debt the Tzeltal Christians owed to their own people would not go unpaid.

Early in February, Florence and I were sitting down to supper, our first opportunity to be alone together for several weeks. The tread of *huaraches* on the stairway interrupted our conversation. Seven young men filed into the room, their serious faces indicating the gravity of their mission.

They sat, very willingly, on chairs which we offered them for they had been on the trail since sun-up. We offered to make them coffee and fry some eggs for them. But until they had told us their message, they would not accept any food though all they had had to eat all day was a gourdful of cold corn gruel.

Domingo Mendez who had attended the Bible School two months before, acted as spokesman for the group.

"*Hermana,*" he said, without the usual preamble of Tzeltal pleasantries, "There are now twelve families in Bahtsibiltic who have believed in God. We have chosen a site to build a chapel. Old Petul Tem, the *trensipal* who gives orders in our area has told us, 'Go to Corralito, and bring the two *gringas* and their medicines to us.' We have come to take you back to Bachajon with us."

There seemed no question in his mind but that we would be eager to drop everything and go.

Florence looked at me and I looked at her. For years we had longed, hoped, prayed, even tried to get our foot in the door at Bachajon only to be discouraged at every attempt. Now seven Bachajon Christians were begging us to enter their home territory.

We reminded them of the potential hazards.

"What if you are ambushed on the trail or have your houses set afire as happened to Santiago for his faith?"

"No matter what happens, we want you to go to Bachajon with us. We want to hear more of God's Word." Each of the seven spoke very firmly.

It had been sixteen years since I had first been refused entry to Bachajon. Now it was God's time.

The uncertainty I had suffered a few months before, after the dedication of the Oxchuc New Testament, was now dissolved. Florence, who had waited so long for her new clinic and who enjoyed it so much, would now be returning to the primitive conditions she had endured for so many years. Typical of her loyalty, she declared without hesitation,

"Where the Lord sends you, I will go, too."

We would be leaving these highland Tzeltals who had become as precious to us as our own family. The parting would be very painful. And still...the call!

We turned to the seven young men awaiting our reply.

"If God's heart wants it to be so," we told them, "we will go back to Bachajon with you after Easter."

Is not My word like a fire?
saith the Lord;
and like a hammer
that breaketh the rock in pieces?
Jeremiah 23:29

It was called,

Bahtsibiltic,

"the place of ferns,"
but it was not home.

Nor would it be
for many difficult weeks.

Chapter Eighteen
Dirt, Dogs and Difficulties

From friendly, open Corralito where Tzeltals swarmed in on us at all hours, included us in all their family affairs and had wept in genuine grief at our leavetaking, we encountered an entirely different breed of Tzeltals. These residents of Bachajon were secretive to the point of hostility. They resented outsiders, even those who came on the invitation of some of their own. Florence with her medicine and I with my Bible, were anything but welcome. The transition was difficult for we had loved our highland Tzeltals and had felt at home with them from the very moment we had arrived in Corralito. Now another adjustment, another calling demanded our attention. We had known it would not be easy and it wasn't.

From the outward view, Bachajon territory was more appealing than Oxchuc country. Tall pine forests with lush tropical growth presented a beauty unknown in the mountains. Exotic flowers grew along the trails while birds of every color flashed from tree to tree in an exhibition of God's versatility in Creation. And it was warm! We had shivered through many highland rainy seasons. Now, we discovered the round open necks of the Indian blouses much more comfortable than our Western clothing.

Bachajon dwellings indicated the nature of their inhabitants. Square, windowless mud huts, roofed with sugarcane leaves which had been blanched by the intense rays of the tropical sun,

each structure stood haughtily aloof from any
other. Disgruntled pigs rooted fruitlessly in the
bushes nearby. Chickens took dustbaths in the
blinding sunlight. Youngsters playing in the dirt
reflected their parents' animosity by refusing to
greet us even when we called out the Bachajon
greeting, *Bohconix.*

"Home" for the first two months was Domingo
Mendez' one room hut. With dry, cracked, mud
walls redolent of wood smoke and earth, some
soot-blackened pots in one corner, a clay griddle
propped against the walls, gourds of assorted
shapes and an egg-shaped water jug with zigzag
lines painted around the middle, it was adequate
for all their needs. Three broken pots turned upside down formed the triangular hearth for the fire.
From the rafters, permanently lacquered with
black soot, hung ears of seedcorn, a few strips of
smoked meat and a circular rack where food was
kept out of reach of the rats. Nearby was heaped
the family's entire supply of corn for the coming
year. In another corner, loose, unplaned boards
laid across poles on forked stakes in the dirt floor
constituted the family bed. Florence and I slept in
our hammocks slung from the rafters.

Near the only doorway stood a long, heavy
bench made out of a log propped on four legs. A
succession of chickens, pigs and dogs paraded in
and out of the house, shooed out as often as they
entered. Until the Indian brethren could get their
cornfields planted and collect poles and thatch for
a house of our own, this would be our home.

Domingo's pretty little wife, xPet (Shpet) welcomed us sweetly. She showed us the nearby
stream hidden among the pine trees where we
could get water, bathe and wash our clothes.
Within a few hours, we had been accepted as part

of the family by sloe-eyed, four-year-old Adela and alert baby Juan, the roving mongrel dogs that were always underfoot and the unruffled setting hen that had appropriated a vacant corner of the hut.

Since food was scarce and we did not want to deprive the young family, we did not eat with them. We had brought our own one-burner stove and cooked separately from them. We were careful, also, to do our own chores so that it would not appear that we expected service. We had come to be of service to them.

Our first night in Bachajon, we were greeted with rumblings of apprehension from the new believers. They had conducted us to their new little chapel just a minute's walk from Domingo's house.

Against a backdrop of tall, stately pines and a massive mountain range shouldering the night sky stood the neatly-thatched little chapel. Twelve of the Indian believers had erected it.

"*Cacique* (chief) Estéban has heard that our sisters have come here to live. His heart is angry."

"Old Petul Tem who sent word to our sisters to come, refuses to come to see them because he fears *cacique* Estéban."

"The *trensipals* in town plan to meet..." This was a threat of witchcraft against the believers.

"Some say they will set fire to our chapel..."

The sober little group of apprehensive new believers squatted on their haunches within the pool of lamplight. In the stillness, we could hear the night wind fingering the thatch of the roof as if desirous of demolishing it.

"What shall I tell them from God's Word?" queried Domingo. I suggested I Peter 2:19-25 for they needed fortification against the tribulation that would most assuredly come. Domingo held his Tzeltal New Testament close to the light radiating from the lantern and began to read. Though he was newly-literate and the words were in a different dialect from his, he persevered until he finished the passage:

It will turn out well for you, if you endure all kinds of bad things done to you because of your faith-of-heart in God. God's heart will be glad about it. Because in the same way Christ passed through suffering for our sakes...

Domingo's clear, confident voice as he explained the words to the rest, dispelled the pall of fear that had shadowed the believers' faces. Heartened by what God had said in His Word and by the fearless faith of Domingo, most of those present affirmed their faith, also. From that moment on, the combined forces of *cacique* Estéban, the *trensipals* and all of Bachajon's superstitions were not enough to quench the Light which had come to the Bachajon forests.

The Bachajon dialect was different from the Oxchuc. We were plunged into the midst of it.

From the vantage point of our hammocks hung in the middle of Domingo's hut, we observed a typical Bachajon family: their concern over the growing corn on which life itself depended, the constant battle against rats eating the corn, army ants swarming the house, possums stealing the chickens, fear of sickness, fear of the supernatural and the gossiping tongues of their neighbors.

From daybreak until late at night, in all situations, we heard Tzeltal spoken. We agreed with Dr. Nida, "There is no substitute for living with and talking constantly with the native users of a language" - even though it meant putting up with dirt, dogs and difficulties!

Each morning, as blackness began to fade into grayness, the whole household wakened to the sounds of the baby crying, chickens clucking and dogs snuffling around the cold ashes of the hearth in search of morsels of food. The acrid smell of woodsmoke told us that xPet had teased the dormant embers of the fire to life again. The day had begun. We dressed inside our sleeping bags in our swaying hammocks which Domingo laughingly called "armadillos' nests."

As more and more people found their way to Domingo's hut on the pretext of visiting their kinsman (but actually to get a closer look at us), Domingo told them about the Lord. He played the Gospel records tirelessly, explained the brightly-colored picture rolls of the Life of Christ to them by the hour and read the Scripture portions to those who could not read. In his eagerness, he reminded me of Martin Gourd in the early days of Yochib. But there were differences.

Domingo was by far the most eloquent speaker I had ever met. He was a born teacher and knowledge flowed out of his lips like a pipe funneling water. He had an outstanding command of the Tzeltal language, with no excess verbiage. An unusually handsome man, with a rugged build, Domingo held a strong influence over his own people. He loved to tell us about the lowland country, the folk tales of his forebears and the various plants and animals and birds about us. I could have asked for no better language teacher.

His own story was fascinating.

I was visiting a schoolteacher who tried to start a school in the settlement of huts called Cacwalha'.

On a board shelf roped to the rafters I found a worn, well-thumbed booklet with the pages coming apart. I could not understand many of the words - it was in another dialect - but I pored over the pictures, wishing someone could tell me more. I wanted the book so much that I paid the fifteen pesos the schoolteacher asked for it...

I broke into his narration with unusual excitement. "We left that booklet in Cacwalha' nine years ago!"

Florence and I had attempted at that time to revive the contacts Bill had made in Bachajon. We had lived for a month with the family of his Indian informant and had left the "Life of Christ" booklet with colored pictures and text in Oxchuc Tzeltal with the Indian family. Once again, God had not allowed His Word to "*return unto Him void!*"

Domingo continued,

I wanted to obey God's Words but there was no one to tell me how. I put the book away and kept on drinking. I drank so heavily that my wife cowered when she saw me, my children fled from me, none of my neighbors dared come near me.

Remembering the painful past, his voice faltered.

One time I went to Ocosingo to buy some salt, a new hat, some earrings for xPet. In my pocket, I had three hundred "pesos" - the price of a cow I had sold. I had made my purchases and was starting for home, when I stopped at the "cantina" for a drink. The next thing I knew, I was in a fistfight with a "mestizo." I looked down to see him sprawled on the stones at my feet. Before the police could get there, I started to run but in my drunkenness, I ran down the wrong road, away from Bachajon, until I fell down in a stupor.

It was pitch dark when I came to my senses. I groped around in the blackness; my new hat was missing. My net bag with a ball of ground-corn had fallen in the mud and someone had stolen the borrowed "huaraches" off my feet. I felt in my pocket for my wad of "pesos." I found only a single fifty-"centavo" piece. Disgusted, I made my way back to town and spent my last fifty "centavos" for another drink. I thought to myself, "Some day you'll fall down in a drunken stupor and never get up again."

The next time I went to Ocosingo, I decided to search for the ones who believe in God and ask them if He could change my heart.

I asked one of the townspeople where they lived. He began to berate me, "What do you want with those devils? Don't have anything to do with them!"

I replied, "If they are devils, as you say they are, I won't have anything to do with them. But tell me where they meet so I can return one of their books to them." With that, he pointed out a group of huts at the edge of town.

I found Antonio, the leader of the congregation, sitting outside his hut. I went up to him and asked, "Are you a believer in God?" He said he was so I requested, "Then tell me what this book says." Instead of giving back the book, I found out what was written in it - the Word of God. That is when I began to believe in God with one heart,

Domingo concluded.

If we had been astounded at the bond of fear the *shamans* held over the Oxchuc Tzeltals, it was increased a hundredfold in Bachajon territory! The old Mayan beliefs had been preserved in less adulterated form than in the highlands and dread of curses was intensified to the point of complete domination of all they did, said or thought. Where

Catholicism in the highlands had modified some of this *shamanism*, its effect was minimal in the lowlands. In fact, within the Catholic church in the town of Bachajon was a Mayan stela which the Bachajon Tzeltals worshipped as well as their patron saint, San Jerónimo.

The kind of "Christianity" which had developed since the days of the Spanish conquerors had incorporated the Mayan beliefs in the supernatural with Christo-pagan concepts. It had not changed their hearts. They still believed each man had a powerful *nagual*, a companion animal spirit. It was necessary they keep secret their *nagual* for fear an enemy should start hunting it. Anyone could be an enemy, even a member of the family.

Of these animal spirits, the jaguar was the most powerful of all *naguals*. The person who possessed a jaguar for his animal spirit could cast a curse of illness or death on others. Even the mention of a jaguar's spirit could strike terror to the heart of an Indian believing he had been cursed. There was no true recourse against this form of sorcery and many times the victim did die.

A constant fear was that of having one's soul "eaten" by the animal spirits. The Bachajontecos believed that animal spirits of the tribal elders wandered through the forest after dark, seeking victims. If a night bird alighted on the roof, the Indians took it for a sign that the animal spirits were abroad. If someone suddenly took ill and died, the animal spirits were blamed. No one knew when he would be the next victim, his soul taken captive, the feathers plucked off and the meat cut up in small pieces for the animal spirits to feast upon.

"Do you see those holes in the thatch roof above the bed?" Domingo asked us one day. For the first time, we noticed that the grass thatch was riddled with small perforations.

"I used to wake up at night in a sweat of terror, too oppressed to cry out, certain that an animal spirit had alighted on the roof in order to 'eat the soul' of someone in my household. I would reach for my shotgun and shoot through the roof. I hoped that if I did not kill the animal spirit, I would at least scare him away until another night."

Domingo himself, he told us, had gained quite a reputation for knowing how to locate the dislodged soul of a sick person by hunting for it with eggs. He had learned how to do it by watching some of the professional "soul-hunters" perform their rites.

I would go to the sick person's hut and look all around for the spot where his soul was likely to be. Then I would take an egg, make a little mound of dirt on the spot and set the egg, small end up, on the mound.

Domingo illustrated by going through the motions of piling up dirt and making the proper incantations.

Then I would make a tiny opening in the top of the egg and peer in. If the eye of the egg appeared in the exact center of the opening, it was a sign that I had located the sick person's soul. If not, I would repeat the whole performance as many times as necessary. Once I found the person's soul, I would call it back into his body and he would get well. I developed a knack for finding sick persons' souls. More and more people sent for me when they were sick and paid me in liquor.

Domingo's healing talents developed in another direction as Florence taught him to give injections, examine specimens under the microscope and dole out pills in carefully-calculated dosages. He became Florence's staunchest ally in explaining to his people that microbes, not animal spirits, caused sickness. When his own son had diarrhea, he ignored his mother's advice to give him ground-up hummingbird and instead, let Florence cure him with a few teaspoonsful of caosol.

For Domingo and xPet, as well as for countless other families in the Bachajon forests, modern medicines, coupled with prayer to a God who hears and heals, brought the first relief from fear of sickness that they had ever known. Domingo told us how sickness and death had harried their lives before they turned to the Lord.

I was twenty, xPet was twelve when I took her home to my hut to be my wife. Our first child was born, a beautiful little girl. When she was barely two weeks old, she became very ill.

"The animal spirits want to eat the soul of this child because she is so beautiful," I told xPet.

"Yes", she agreed in despair. "One's first child is always eaten by the animal spirits."

But I rebelled. "We will not let them eat her soul," I told her. We hurried off to the town of Bachajon to find someone with power to save her life. I gave the healer two bottles of liquor to take the child's pulse and find out who had cast a curse on her. He drank the liquor immediately, listened to her pulse between spasms of coughing and told us, "Go on home. She'll get well." We believed him. We started home but halfway there she stopped breathing. I was furious. I wanted to kill him. But xPet dissuaded me.

There was anguish in both the young parents' faces as they recalled their grief. Domingo continued,

When our second child was born, I found a man with a powerful animal spirit, a jaguar, to be her godfather. He promised to protect her with his magical power. Each year, I gave him my fattest pig and spent most of my money to buy liquor for him in return for his protecting my child. Even so, she became ill.

Adela, squatting beside her mother to help shell corn into a wicker basket was listening wide-eyed to her father's tale.

To protect her from the animal spirits that wanted to eat her soul, I held her in my arms all night and kept the fire blazing furiously. Still she did not get well.

In desperation, xPet and I finally abandoned our hut and slept on the open mountainside night after night. "The animal spirits won't find us here," we told one another. And all the time, I was saying in my heart, "If this child dies too, I'll kill the one who cast a curse on her." But she did not die. I found some herbs and gave them to her to drink and, little by little, she got better.

Domingo was close to tears as he concluded,

It hurts to be in the hand of the devil.

With a more impelling sense of urgency than ever, we kept at our task of translating God's Word into Bachajon dialect. Though not a completely different language from the highland Tzeltal, the grammar and vocabulary had marked differences. The sociolinguistic implications were important for the Bachajon considered the highland dialect "mutilated" from their own. They thought of themselves as the elite of the Tzeltals and would not have read a book written in Oxchuc dialect. Following the example of our earlier years in Corralito, we used more than one helper at a time with

Domingo as the principal informant and others listening in to criticize and correct.

Florence held reading classes for the men and boys each afternoon so they would be ready to read their own Scriptures when they came in printed form. We began translation of the Gospel of Luke.

In the course of our translating, we came to the story of the sinful woman who anointed Jesus' feet in the house of Simon. I related the story to Domingo in highland Tzeltal; Simon's niggardliness toward the Lord, the woman's brokenness before the Lord and the Lord's touching exoneration,

Her sins, which are many, are forgiven, for she loved much...

Domingo stopped, his brow furrowed in concentration. There was a long silence. I looked up. Tears coursed down Domingo's bronzed face. He wiped them away with the back of his hand.

"I am just like that woman," he admitted brokenly. "My sins are many, too. Before I heard God's Word, I was just like a dog."

At the remembrance of the sinfulness and sordidness of his past life, tears again flowed unchecked down his cheeks.

"I have sinned much. But Christ has lost my sins out of his heart. That is why I love Him so much," Domingo finished. Time and again, he was to prove how greatly he loved the One Who had forgiven him much.

We had been living in Domingo's hut for six weeks, each day expecting the distant rumblings of protest on the part of the *trensipals* to develop into a full-blown storm. Our greatest safeguard was that we were living in the home of a leading Bachajon man like Domingo Mendez. No one had lifted a hand against us so far.

One night, we were wakened by the frantic barking of the dogs. With the heart-stopping fear that unseen enemies might be surrounding the hut in the starless night, I lay in my hammock waiting for someone to make the first move. It was four-thirty, just before dawn. With the snarling dogs barking a crescendo of warning, Domingo rose and went to the doorway, setting aside the upright planks which served as a door. At a sharp order from Domingo, the barking subsided into frustrated growls. Then a voice called out in a conciliatory tone,

"*Hermano*" (brother).

I recognized the voice of Sebastian Cruz. He came to stand right before Domingo's doorway where we could hear his tale clearly.

"Is it true, *hermano*, that our sisters have been killed?" he asked in an anxious voice. "Some of our *mestizo* brethren read in the newspapers that an Oxchuc Indian killed our sister Marianna for forcing him to believe. Then he cut her up in little pieces."

Safe inside the downy comfort of my sleeping bag, I listened to a lurid account of my untimely demise announced in the two major newspapers of the state capitol the day before, *Diario de Chiapas* and *Voz del Suroeste*. A phrase of the Apostle Paul popped into my mind with new meaning and I smiled to myself.

As dying, and behold we live!

Domingo put a reassuring hand on Sebastian's shoulder. "*Hermano*, both of our sisters are perfectly safe. They are asleep in their hammocks inside my hut."

We were touched by the deep concern of Sebastian and those who had urged him to investigate our wellbeing. He had traveled all day from far-off Yajalon to his home where he had heard the news, and then he had walked another two hours through the night to Domingo's hut.

By some erroneous deduction, the story had circulated that since we were no longer at Corralito, we must have been killed. Like most stories of this kind, it was easier to spread a rumor than to discover the truth.

Somehow, that example of anxious love from Sebastian who had traveled so far that day just to see about us, supplied the sense of belonging we had needed. We were no longer strangers in Bachajon.

*My Word shall accomplish
that which I please,
and prosper in the thing
whereto I sent it.*
                    Isaiah 55:11

We stared
at the formidable pile of rocks,
unbelievingly.

"It's there, *hermana.* See?"

Manuel led the way.

And then we saw it,
a small opening
between piled-up boulders,
which easily escaped the casual observer.

Chapter Nineteen

From Terror To Triumph

A cave indeed - one which had been hidden for centuries. Like earthworms, we squirmed our way through a long black tunnel of earth, mildewed rocks and spider webs till we reached the cavernous space where we could at last take standing positions. It was my first authentic viewing of an ancient Mayan worship center. I had studied the culture and architecture of the proud ancestors of these Tzeltals but had never actually been in one of their present-day closely-guarded sites of worship. Rock slides caused by an earthquake had hidden the entrance to all but a few knowing Indians. I was more excited than I indicated by my outward demeanor.

I turned my flashlight on a large boulder which lay horizontally across the center of the cave. On it was outlined in durable black paint a seated Mayan figure in profile, somewhat smaller than life-size. Typical of the art work of that time, he sat crosslegged with an intricate headdress adorning his head. The hieroglyphs on the right bottom of the stone probably dated back to around 700 A.D. - over 1200 years ago! Quickly, with Florence holding the flashlight, I copied the drawing as closely as possible. We were doubtless the only North Americans ever to see that particular Mayan memorial to times past. I wanted to linger, taking in everything. But with the rocks piled so loosely about us, any stray misstep by ourselves or the Indians with us could trap us inside and cause a disaster. We had posted a lookout at the entrance but with no earthmoving equipment in the vicinity, we dared not linger long. It had been a momentous event for me to see the actual place where Mayans had memorialized an ancient god, for I had studied this culture for years, digesting anything written on the subject and cultivating the acquaintance of archaeologists who specialized in the subject.

Long romanticized as a scientifically-advanced people of peace, Mayan culture was in truth more cruel. Self-mutilation, warfare on neighboring city-states and protracted torture of captives were common practice among these ancestors of the Tzeltals. Ancient ball games pitted captives against one another, with the head of the loser used in some secret rite to the gods. Hallucinations of serpents were induced in order to contact either the gods or the dead. Prince killed prince for access to the throne. For its time, Mayan civilization had been surprisingly advanced technologically. And yet, the heart of the people without Christ had been no different than the many generations of descendants since. All of them had passed into Eternity without relief from sorrow, dread and blackness.

We emerged into the bright sunlight, shuddering at the contrast. At a short distance stood the newly-erected chapel. A school had been started in that tiny settlement. Medical assistance was available in the district. The Word was spreading. And there were thousands more to be told.

It was a violent family in a violent society. Murders by witchcraft, *machete*, poison and guns shadowed the Cruz family from generation to generation. Feuds flared, brother killed brother, a whole family was chopped to pieces.

It was from such a family that Manuel came. He was a bright fourteen-year-old, a student at the government boarding school when Bill Bentley visited his village of Bachajon in 1939. Manuel was drawn to the fair-skinned foreigner out of curiosity. He spoke Tzeltal far better than any *mestizo* could. But the message of Eternal Life which Bill brought did not interest the teenager. He was more interested in the affairs of this life.

Manuel went on to complete sixth grade and trade school as well, eventually returning to his own tribe with an outward veneer of education but none of his inward fears eradicated. The threat of witchcraft and of evil spirits darkened his life.

He became a government teacher for eight years and traveled from place to place to establish schools. He possessed knowledge but no peace of heart. He had many women. He became involved with hard-drinking friends many of whom carried pistols. As a sideline, he began to sell liquor. He lived a life of constant terror from enemies he made and from the curses cast on him.

He took a wife. Their first two children died despite all they could do to pay the *shamans*. His wife became ill and Manuel sought the jurisdiction of *shamans* with more magical power. He gave them his cows and horses. Juana eventually recovered but Manuel was left with nothing.

Then he received a Book. It had belonged to his brother Sebastian's son. When the young man lay dying, he said to his father,

It doesn't matter if I die. But as for you, pay attention to what God says in His Word. I leave you my Bible. Take it to my Uncle Manuel. He knows how to read. He knows Spanish. Maybe he, too, will believe in God.

It was a small book and it was in Spanish for the Bible had not yet been translated into Tzeltal. But Manuel began to read. Gradually, the Light of the Word began to dawn on him. He realized he must understand how to believe in God. From a Christian who did not know how to read, Manuel learned there were believers in Corralito. He asked if any of them could come to him and explain what the Book meant. Three of the elders from Corralito responded to his appeal, staying in his house long enough to teach heartsick Manuel how to believe and obey the Lord. God's Word, not education, had dispelled Manuel's terrors. From that time on, he became the greatest helper we had for our translation work.

The Bachajontecos had built us a house of our own, one just like theirs, in the clearing where the chapel stood. It was unpretentious in style but one in which they felt comfortable to visit. Near the door stood a bench which was almost always filled with visitors, big and little. Here they felt free to look at the picture books, play the Gospel records endlessly, even spit on the dirt floor. Close to our hut stood an abandoned corncrib. Manuel appropriated this rude shelter for his family and moved in to be close to Florence and me to help with the translation. With his education and quick mind, he became invaluable in the work we felt impelled to do as rapidly as possible.

More and more, Domingo Mendez had become involved in pastoral work for his people. It was to his leadership they turned with their problems, much as the Corralito believers had turned to Juan Mucha. He kept so busy in talking to people about the Lord that he had little time for such mundane tasks as gathering firewood until his wife threatened to serve him uncooked food!

With these two outstanding co-workers, we began to see a quick growth in the Bachajon believers. Of course, Florence and I had been through many of the same experiences in the years previous and had learned to simplify and speed much of our task. Yet it never seemed repetitious. Each new day brought fresh joy and challenge.

New days also brought threats, for Satan would not allow his territory to be claimed without a struggle. *Cacique* Estéban, the chief of all the Bachajon territory, continued to threaten the Christians. Once he met Domingo on the trail and pistol-whipped him for teaching "the Devil's words." Domingo stood firm.

Enemies threatened to set fire to his hut or to exercise witchcraft against him and his family, or to kill him in ambush on the trail. He staunchly affirmed that he had been set free from such terror and refused to display any alarm.

Others turned to the Lord through his fearless testimony and through the first portions of Scripture he helped translate. The triumph of his simple trust was an example many emulated.

Still, in spite of *cacique* Estéban's name being a familiar one throughout Bachajon, neither Florence nor I had ever laid eyes on him. We knew his word was law in the territory, more so than that of the state governor in the distant capital. He had gained his ascendancy over his fellow-Indians partly by native shrewdness, partly by knowing more Spanish than anyone else. He had discarded his Indian wife in favor of a Spanish-speaking señora, carried a pistol on his hip and lived in a house with a sheet-metal roof, all indications of a rise in the world but only by means of trampling on his fellow-Indians.

One day, when we had been living in our house for about a year, a stranger on a strong roan horse rode slowly into our clearing, dismounting stiffly as if in considerable pain. Domingo whispered to me in awed excitement,

"It's *cacique* Estéban!"

The slender, sickly-looking man in *mestizo* clothes came toward us. He doffed his hat in an un-Indian flourish and spoke to us courteously.

"I have come to consult you. I have been quite sick and I heard you have medicines here."

"Yes, we have," I assured him. "We will be glad to be of whatever service we can to you."

My heart beat hard at the opportunity the Lord was giving us to win the foremost opponent of the Gospel. I ushered him into our hut, half of which served as a dispensary. It was obvious that our hut was less imposing than his own; he could see that we had not come to usurp land which belonged to the Indians. Florence diagnosed his ailment and gave him medication; he saw that we were there to serve him and his fellow-Tzeltals.

Even after he had received his medicine, Estéban seemed in no hurry to leave. He sat on our Bachajon bench, legs crossed, chatting with Domingo and me. I marveled at the sweet absence of revenge in Domingo who still bore the scars from the pistol-whipping Estéban had given him a few months before. It was as if it had never occurred.

For once, no other visitor came to the door, no one brought eggs to sell, no one asked for medicine. For the space of an hour or more, we talked to Estéban about the Lord. It could quite possibly be his only opportunity to hear. With his head slightly bent, he listened attentively for the first time to the Word of God he had so adamantly opposed. It was hard to believe that this courteous gentleman had once given the order for the first Bachajon believer to be killed.

I opened the Tzeltal New Testament to the third chapter of John and read to him about another chieftain.

Don Estéban, long ago there was a cacique like you, named Nicodemus. He came to the Lord Jesus by night because he knew he needed his heart changed by God.

Domingo humbly added his own testimony of what God had done in his heart and in the life of his family.

Finally, reluctantly, even wistfully, the ailing *cacique* got up to leave.

"We would like to give you this Book as a gift," I told him, holding out the New Testament. It was a two-column edition with Spanish on one side and Tzeltal on the other. "In it you can read for yourself in Spanish or in your own language, Tzeltal, what God has put into writing for us. May God's Words enter your heart."

He stood immobile for a few seconds while we held our breath, not knowing if he would accept the copy of God's Book. He took it in his hand, thanked us graciously and said goodbye.

Never again did *cacique* Estéban raise a hand against the believers. The way had been cleared for the Word of God to "*have free course, and be glorified*" throughout all of Bachajon.

When Estéban's hostility against Christian influence in Bachajon ceased, the word reached the Governor of the State of Chiapas, Dr. Samuel Leon Brindis, that some of the Bachajon Indians, whose reputation for brutality had formerly kept outsiders from entering their territory, were now law-abiding citizens. He wanted to see for himself. With a party of four, Dr. Leon Brindis inspected the new school the Indian Christians were building on their own initiative, examined the orderly, well-stocked clinic that was ministering to hundreds in the area and attended a service in the thatch-roofed chapel. We gave him a copy of the highland Tzeltal New Testament which had transformed so many Tzeltal lives. One of his party departed with a pistol sticking out of one hip pocket and a Tzeltal hymnal out of the other! The governor was amazed for a few short years before, he would have feared to set foot in that area. His people had seen a Great Light.

It was in May, 1965, that the first shipment of newly-printed Bachajon New Testaments was flown into the Bahtsibiltic clearing. The little thatch-roofed chapel of years before had been exchanged for a spacious solidly-built church with a handsome portico which the Bachajon Christians themselves had constructed. Hundreds gathered from all over the region for the dedication service. At the end, they crowded forward, eager hands reaching for their own copy of God's Word. By the end of the day, there were very few copies left. These formerly-unreached Tzeltals of the Bachajon pine forests finally had in their hands "the Book from God" which old Miguel de Mesa had requested of Bill Bentley so many years before!

The terror of the past had become the triumph of the present.

Yea, so have I strived
to preach the gospel,
not where Christ was named.
Romans 15:20

He was an extraordinary man
in an ordinary body.

Of medium height and weight,
there was little about his appearance
to indicate the immense influence
this humble man
would have on my personal life,
or on that of missions throughout the world.

Chapter Twenty

Uncle Cam

William Cameron Townsend was a true visionary. He was a generation ahead of his time. Ideas flowed from him as if directly channeled from on high.

Somehow, when Uncle Cam made a suggestion, courteously, almost in an offhand manner, it was as if the idea had been planted, allowed to germinate, then had sprung up when the time was ripe, to produce undreamed-of fruit. We who plodded along one task at a time, needed a leader who could see into the future with the vast scope of possibilities opened as if they were already accomplishments.

I first met him at Camp Wycliffe in 1940. Conditions there were rustic and provided the setting for close family ties which never left us. Uncle Cam's enthusiasm sparked us all. He lived, breathed, talked Bible translation. He permeated the camp with his excitement. His animation stimulated us so that we couldn't wait to get started.

When Bill died just before our wedding and I had timidly asked if I could still go to the Tzeltals, he had been the only one with enough confidence to back me up in my commitment to the people for whom Bill cared so deeply. Others had insisted I should enter a tribe where work was already begun. But Uncle Cam overruled all the other opinions and permitted me to go where I was certain God had called me.

Through the years of missionary life in Mexico, Uncle Cam kept us aware that he was always praying for us. Sometimes in the midst of a conversation, he would squint his eyes and assume an "other-worldly" expression. We knew he was praying for all aspects of the conversation - past, present and future. And still, he was fun to be with. He laughed as easily as he talked about Bible translation. No lofty intellectual, he maintained conversation on a comfortable level. He kept in close personal touch with letters, encouraging, advising but always treating each of us as if we were much-loved members of his own family.

His sympathy for family concerns was constant. In 1955, I was at home in Philadelphia with my elderly, ailing parents for an extended period of time. I occupied my days with proofreading the nearly-finished Oxchuc New Testament while I remained on call to assist them when they needed. Uncle Cam called one day on the phone.

"I'm in Philadelphia for a short time," he said. "We have a small gathering scheduled here in the home of Cal Rensch's parents. Would you be willing to say a word or two about your work with the Tzeltals?"

How could anyone refuse this wonderful gentleman?

Then he added, almost as an afterthought, "Do you think you could tell them that you are willing to serve the Lord in yet another place when you are finished with this New Testament?"

I had the next few hours in which to make a momentous decision - to continue work among the Tzeltals whom I dearly loved or to say "Yes" to leaving them and going to others in need of God's

Word in their own language. It was not an easy choice.

Following the meeting that evening, after publicly expressing my willingness to go on to another tribal group, I asked in some curiosity, "Uncle Cam, what country did you have in mind for me to go to next?"

His eyes took on a faraway look as he gazed beyond me.

"How about Colombia?" he said.

Colombia, South America! That was at the height of the years of "The Violence" in that strife-ridden country where 200,000 people were killed by their own countrymen in the cruelest of fashions. It did not seem a likely place for two single women in fairly frail health to go.

Such practical considerations never deterred Uncle Cam. He went on to explain that a French linguist had completed a survey and his data revealed that possibly 136 language groups existed in Colombia. Uncle Cam saw beyond the political turmoil to the day when Colombia would allow foreigners to enter its territory and minister to the Indian tribes who had never heard the Gospel.

Uncle Cam was convinced that each tribe could be stimulated to concern for others and thus propagate the Gospel within their own country themselves. It was a principle which had been proven true among the Tzeltals for they had already begun their missionary outreach to other tribes. Among these were the Tzotzils and the Tojolabals. He also felt there was a danger when missionaries lingered too long in a tribe, that they might stifle the spiritual growth of the indigenous peoples who needed the independence

of making their own decisions and heading their
own churches and Bible schools.

He set the pattern for Wycliffe policy for each
team was encouraged to move on when their New
Testament had been completed and was in use. It
was an excellent principle since translation
speeded with experience. The Oxchuc New Testament had taken us fifteen years to complete; the
Bachajon New Testament in a related dialect, required only six.

Colombia would not open its borders to missionaries. There was tremendous hostility toward
evangelicals of any kind. Then in 1958, Uncle
Cam received an invitation from a close friend to
fly up from Mexico to North Carolina to meet the
Ambassador from Colombia at the friend's home.
It was from this contact, and the influence this
Ambassador wielded, that Uncle Cam was given
his opening to renew negotiations with the Colombian government. At first, they were willing to
allow a contract with the Summer Institute of Linguistics if we would promise not to translate the
Bible into the Indian languages.

"But that is the purpose of our whole existence,"
Uncle Cam insisted. He would not sign a contract
without this important point included. Then, in
1962, Alberto Lleras Camargo, President of
Colombia, finally signed a contract with the Summer Institute of Linguistics in which we were given
permission to pursue translation work. President
Lleras Camargo left office that year and if we had
not secured the contract then, we probably would
not have for many more years.

In the meantime, Florence and I had spent
several years among the Bachajon Tzeltals, the
area I had wanted to enter many years before with
Bill Bentley. The Lord, in His lovingkindness, had

allowed us to see that seed bearing fruit before we were to answer the call to yet another land.

We had nearly finished our translation of the Bachajon New Testament when Uncle Cam paid a visit to the Tzeltal believers both in the highlands of Oxchuc and in Bachajon territory. His request of the Tzeltal Christians was very simple.

"You have received the Gospel from God and you have His Word in your language. Would you be willing to send Marianna and Florence to another country so that others, too, might hear?"

Again, as always, how could anyone refuse such a courteously-worded request from such a humble servant of the Lord?

With much heart-searching, they prayed. The Tzeltal believers consented to send us on.

We prepared to leave for yet another country, another group of Indians for whom our Savior died. We were torn at leaving these people who had become so dear to our hearts. But our task here was accomplished. Two major dialects of the Tzeltals had received the Book in their own language. The Good Seed had been planted. It would yield fruit for many generations to come.

Fresh challenges lay ahead.

I will gather all nations and tongues,
and they shall come and see My glory.
Isaiah 66:18

A pair of hawks circled lazily
in the Mexican sky,
brilliantly clear
in the last stage of dry season.

The corn, dark green and fertile,
fairly burst out of the earth
in a celebration
of growth and abundance.

Fifty-foot trees shaded the hillsides
where once had been little
but barren landscape
and stubby grass.

Corralito was changed,
and Corralito was the same.

We were home again.

Chapter Twenty-one

Twenty Years Later

The van in which we were riding lurched a little in the ruts of the steep road. Florence and I marvelled at its very existence for it had been nothing but a foot path when we had left so many years before. The roads were thronged with hundreds of well-wishers in their brightly-embroidered Tzeltal clothing. Where had they all come from? Had we known all of these people? How had the word spread so quickly that we were coming back?

Other things had changed as well. Once-young faces were now middle-aged and the middle-aged had become strangely wrinkled. In our excitement, we strained hard to remember them all for they were dear, familiar faces; the same wonderful Indians we had loved so well. We prayed the language would come back to us and it did. Phrases we had long forgotten came fluidly to our lips as if awaiting their recall.

It had been twenty long years. Florence and I had been high in the Colombian Andes working with the Paez Indians. Now the New Testament was completed in the Paez language, thanks to the willingness of these Tzeltal Indians to send us out in order that others, too, might hear. With us from Colombia had come Paez Pastor Porfirio Ocaña, holding the recently-published Paez New Testament in his hand to demonstrate the gratitude of his people for the Tzeltals' willingness to share. They had not been easy years for us but hardest of all had been the break from our Tzeltal family over whom we had yearned and agonized, with whom we had laughed and loved and prayed. The Tzeltals were our first love. We had never forgotten them nor had we dreamed that one day we would be welcomed back by such joyous celebration.

Men, wearing Western garb for the most part, lined both sides of the road, calling to us with familiar Tzeltal greetings. Women, in their gaily decorated *huipils*, hair neatly combed, stretched out their arms to hand us gifts of eggs. Children grinned shyly from the shoulders of their proud fathers, urged to look at the *me'tiks* who had brought the Gospel many years before they were born. Florence unabashedly allowed tears to run down her cheeks while I was overwhelmed with the outpouring of love from these who had remained faithful to the Lord through all the years. Indeed, they had not only remained faithful in their own families but they had spread His Word through all the Tzeltal region.

Our visit was limited to only a few days and we had not much time to spend with anyone. We travelled throughout Tzeltal territory, visiting as many congregations as we could, each one celebrating as joyfully as any homecoming could ever be. Time after time, we were approached by an Indian, tears filling his eyes, who repeated his gratitude for our bringing his people the Word. We had not known if we would even be remembered but the welcome given us was from full and grateful hearts. Individual lives had been changed and Tzeltal life as a whole had been revolutionized.

When we had left in 1965, there were 72 congregations of Tzeltal believers. Now, in 1985, there were 322. When we had left, there were over 6,000 believers. Now there were some 44,000 on the church rolls, including children. Where music had been used only for drunken festivities, now well-played guitars and accordions added much to every Christian gathering. The believers had learned to sing in harmony and had even written some of their own hymns.

Not only their spiritual life had been affected. Over 80 well-equipped medical clinics were manned by Tzeltal paramedics, caring for their own people. Women, who had never been allowed to do anything but care for their homes and fields, were now heading up some of these clinics as nurses accredited by the government. The population had tripled because of lower infant mortality rates and better sanitation methods. Young people were going on for further education, taking up careers undreamed of by their parents. In spite of many of the younger people having learned Spanish, they maintained their use of Tzeltal with an intense pride in their tribal identity. They were now not only Tzeltals but Mexican citizens; no longer considered "dogs" but worthy of respect and courtesy.

My memory travelled back through those early years to some of the Tzeltals I had first known. Maria, my companion and helper in my first days in Yochib who had suffered so much from fear of evil spirits and the power of the *shamans*, had died. Her daughter, Maruch, was in the crowd that greeted us. She was now a mature Christian with a family who had grown up without the superstition and dread their grandmother had known.

Martin Gourd, our first evangelist, had also died but his wife greeted us with broad smiles and fond greetings. This was the woman who had been beaten because she did not want to leave "the old ways." Martin had learned better since. Their daughter, Regina, had married Juan Lopez Balte, the schoolboy in Yochib who had believed despite severe beatings from his parents and teacher. Juan had evangelized Tenejapa and Cancuc in his early adult years. Now, he was an excellent clinic worker and he and Regina were the parents of ten healthy children who also followed the Lord.

Maria Kituk who had given birth to her baby in the plane, had died and Tomás still grieved over her. He had married again, though, and had two more children from his second marriage. He was in charge of the government-sponsored clinic near Corralito which had expanded its work tremendously.

Francisco Nimail, the former schoolteacher, was the faithful pastor of the Corralito church now numbering 4,000 members. When we first arrived at the church, it was difficult to realize that this fine modern edifice with its handsome arched facade and Sunday School addition had been preceded thirty-five years ago by a simply-constructed building of reed walls and thatched roof. Now each chapel in the area had a name taken from the Bible: Bethany, Palestine, Nazareth. The one at Corralito was called Golgotha.

Manuel Cruz was now sixty-two and the pastor of several congregations in Bachajon. He and Francisco between them had been instrumental in translating the Old Testament into Tzeltal and were getting it ready for press.

Juan Mucha had not received word that we had returned. We were disappointed not to see him for he had meant so much to us through the early years at Corralito. But Domingo Mucha, his cousin, was there and told us proudly that he was now working in the government clinic in Oxchuc.

I wish I could say that Juan Nich, our old-time foe, had since given his heart to the Lord but he never did. We were told that he was a sad figure, bitter and cruel, for he had hardened his heart against the Gospel for many years.

Old Marcos Ensin with his chieftain's demeanor came, representing the people of Pakwina. Not looking much older than he had on our last visit twenty years ago, he was as dignified as ever. His family had remained faithful to the Lord and had prospered.

Prosperity seemed to have become a corollary to Christianity. These Indians, formerly so poor they could not afford shoes, now lived in whitewashed houses with several rooms. One man was even the proud owner of two trucks. Now that the Tzeltals no longer drank, they could keep the money they earned to spend on needs as well as a few luxuries. Some no longer used the "slash and burn" method of farming and their crops had expanded to include much more than corn. They had learned to cultivate coffee, operate small stores and run businesses. We were amazed at their success. Several times, a Tzeltal would call us aside and give us a gift because the Lord had prospered him financially as well as spiritually.

Not everyone had remained faithful, of course. As in every church throughout the centuries, there were a few who had turned back to the attractions of the world about them. Domingo Mendez, the golden-tongued orator from Bahtsibiltic, was one of these. It wounded us deeply to hear this for he had been specially gifted of God in pastoral care and preaching. But in the places of these few had risen men and women staunch for God, fervent in their desire to obey Him and spread His good news to others.

The days of our brief visit were occupied with formal and informal welcomes. Don Porfirio endeared himself to the hearts of the Tzeltals with his humble manner and grateful words. Florence and I were given so many *huipils* we would never have had to buy clothes again if we had decided to attire ourselves in Tzeltal garb alone.

Where once we had faced nothing but heartbreak and disappointment, now we saw one-fourth of the Tzeltals as true believers. Was it worth the cost? Or the sacrifice of Bill Bentley's life?

Except a corn of wheat
fall into the ground and die,
it abideth alone:
but if it die,
it bringeth forth much fruit.
(John 12:24).

With reluctant hearts, we bade our beloved Tzeltals goodbye. Both Florence and I would willingly relive all those years we spent among them. We cannot.

We must be content that. . .

we planted "the Good Seed,"

others who came after us watered it,

but God gave the increase.